To:

_____

From:

_____

Those who hope in the LORD
will renew their strength.
They will soar on wings like eagles....

Isaiah 40:31

         ZondervanPublishingHouse
         Grand Rapids, Michigan 49530
         http//www.zondervan.com

Published under license from ZondervanPublishingHouse
Design: Mark Veldheer
Cover photograph © Jeremy Walker/Tony Stone Images
Interior photography by Jeremy Walker/Tony Stone Images, Digital Stock, Eyewire Images,
Photodisc, Morey Milbradt/Artville and Mark Veldheer.

Developed exclusively for ZondervanPublishingHouse by The Livingstone Corporation.
00 01 02 03 04 05 06 / HK / 9 8 7 6 5 4 3 2

stories
of
HOPE
for a
healthy
SOUL

Hallmark
BOOKS

📖 Zondervan

BOK 3022

Contents

LOOK AHEAD

LOOK BEYOND

PERSPECTIVE, POINT OF VIEW, A WAY OF LOOKING and seeing—
your perspective makes all the difference.

Looking down, the view is limited. Focusing on this world and human
endeavor, you can feel overwhelmed by the seeming futility of life. Solomon had
it right: "Meaningless! Meaningless! Utterly meaningless! Everything is meaningless" (Ecclesiastes 1:2). No wonder people sell their souls for prestige, power,
or possessions . . . if nothing else matters.

During the desert temptation, Satan had Jesus look down from the mountain
top. "All this I will give you if you will bow down and worship me"

(Matthew 4:9), he promised. That would be a strong temptation to anyone
looking down on the nation below. But Jesus looked up and rejected Satan,
knowing that reality lay beyond the earth, beyond the planets and stars . . . and
all of those were already his. How could this finite world compare with an
infinite God? There is no comparison. The choice was easy.

When you feel as though you are losing your grip and losing hope, perhaps
it's because you are looking down. Turn your head, take your eyes off this earth,
change your perspective and look up. See that your all-powerful, all-knowing,
and all-loving God is in control, and he cares for you. TAKE HOPE.

MY HOPE IS BUILT

Edward Mote and William B. Bradbury

MY HOPE is built on nothing less than Jesus' blood and righteousness;
I dare not trust the sweetest frame, but wholly lean on Jesus' name.

On Christ the solid Rock I stand; All other ground is sinking sand,
All other ground is sinking sand.

When darkness veils his lovely face, I rest on His unchanging grace;
In every high and stormy gale, my anchor holds within the veil.

On Christ the solid Rock I stand; All other ground is sinking sand,
All other ground is sinking sand.

His oath, His covenant, His blood, support me in the whelming flood;
When all around my soul gives way, He then is all my hope and stay.

On Christ the solid Rock I stand; All other ground is sinking sand,
All other ground is sinking sand.

When He shall come with trumpet sound, O may I then in Him
be found:
Dressed in His righteousness alone, faultless to stand before the throne.

On Christ the solid Rock I stand; All other ground is sinking sand,
All other ground is sinking sand.

THE SWEETNESS OF GOD'S LOVE
Marilyn Meberg

KEN AND I GOT MARRIED when I had just turned twenty-two and he twenty-three. We felt very mature and eager to begin married life together. . . . Two years after we were married, we had a baby, a boy. Two years later, true to plan, we had another baby, a girl.

But my euphoria after the effortless birth of little Joanie was short-lived. There was a problem, the doctor tried to explain to us, and it was serious. Joanie was born with spina bifida, a defect of the spine in which part of the spinal cord and spinal fluid are exposed through a gap in the backbone. This defect was more life-threatening in the sixties than it is now. At best, her life would be characterized by many operations and hospital stays but never normal living.

I really couldn't grasp what Dr. Webster was saying. I'd never heard of spina bifida, and besides, it wasn't in the plan. . . .

Then, on the fifteenth day of her life, we encountered another even sharper curve. Joanie died of spinal meningitis, a complication from her spina bifida. She had never come home from the hospital. I had never even held her in my arms.

I set about trying to make sense of it all. That's what I frequently try to do with really sharp curves. . . . But this kind of strategy is an attempt to do the impossible. Life often doesn't make sense; God often doesn't make sense. In this situation, what did make sense was the reward that was mine after maneuvering the sharp curve. I'll never be the same.

One morning, a number of months after Joanie died, I sat in my bedroom with my Bible on my lap. I love the Psalms and frequently meander around in them; sometimes with a specific purpose but often just because I like going there. On this particular morning, I found myself in Psalm 62.

I was reading along with some measure of indifference until I came to verse 11: "One thing God has spoken, two things have I heard: that you, O God, are strong, and that you, O Lord, are loving."

Whoa! "That you, O God, are strong." Yes, strong enough to have healed Joanie . . . but you didn't. Strong enough to have prevented the defect

in the first place . . . but you didn't. Strong enough to heal any of your children . . . sometimes you do and sometimes you don't. All of this I do not understand.

This was a crossroads on my journey: I could rail against God for what he did and did not do. I could be bitter, lose my faith, or more realistically, just become a whiner. On the other hand, I could heed the following phrase, "You, O Lord, are loving."

As a preacher's kid, I was taught biblical truths both at home and in church. One of the foundational truths I heard over and over was that Jesus loved me. It was the first song I ever learned to sing. And now, it was as if the message "Jesus loves me" that started in my youth had gathered snowball momentum until it literally rolled all over me that morning. "You, O Lord, are loving."

What a liberating truth! I do not now nor will I ever have all the answers for my many imponderable questions about God. But that morning he rewarded me with the sweet knowledge of his love in a way I had not previously experienced. It softened me, it satisfied me, and it served as a salve for my bleeding soul.

A Spirit that Soars

Dave and Jan Dravecky

TRACY KEETH USED TO BE QUITE AN ATHLETE. In junior high she played basketball, volleyball, and softball. All that came to an end in high school, however, when Reiter's syndrome (a rare form of arthritis) caused severe pain and swelling in her legs.

"I had headaches just from clenching my teeth to fight back the pain," Tracy said. Her condition forced her to spend much of her senior year at home, and in 1992 doctors amputated her right leg. She fought to regain a normal life, but a little more than a year after she lost one leg, doctors were forced to take the other. By this point, if you tried to make a judgment on her "inside" by watching what was happening on her "outside," you'd be making a grave error. In fact, while her body was suffering, her spirit was soaring.

"I haven't been a committed Christian all of my life," Tracy admits. "It's a shame that it takes something like this to bring us closer to God, but that is what happened to me. When I was in so much pain that I couldn't sleep, I spent a great deal of time reading the Bible and in prayer." One night, when the pain was overwhelming, she began thinking how nice it would be to die. But in the same instant she began thinking about the pain Jesus suffered when he was beaten, spit upon, and crucified. And she knew she wanted to know Jesus more intimately than she ever had.

"I have lived life when I really didn't know God," Tracy says, "and I've lived life when I can't get enough of him. I've seen both sides of the fence. Now that I know him, I can't help but smile when I think about what he has done in my life."

GOD'S BEAUTIFUL WORLD

Barbara Johnson

THE DAY HAD NOT STARTED OUT WELL for a certain woman. She had overslept and was late for work. Then some things happened at the office that only contributed to her harried condition. By the time she reached the bus stop for her trip home, her stomach was tied in an intricate knot. As usual, the bus was late and packed, and she had to stand up. The bus started, stopped, turned left, then right, pushing and pulling her in all directions. The day wasn't improving even as it came to an end.

Then she heard a man's voice up front proclaim, "Beautiful day, isn't it?"

Because of the crowd she couldn't see the man, but he continued to comment on everything the bus passed that added to his joy: a church here, an ice cream store there, a baseball diamond here, a library there. The atmosphere in the bus grew immediately more carefree, as did the woman's heart. The man's enthusiasm was so winsome, the woman found herself smiling. When the bus reached the woman's stop, she worked her way through the crowd to the door. As she did so, she glanced at the "tour guide"—a plump man, wearing dark glasses and carrying a white cane. He was blind.

As she stepped off the bus, she realized the day's tensions had disappeared. God had sent a blind man to help her see that, though things go wrong sometimes, it's still a beautiful world.

GOD IS ABLE

Philip Yancey

NOT LONG AFTER READING the books by
Elie Wiesel and Corrie ten Boom, I visited the
site of one of the Nazi concentration camps. On
the grounds of the Dachau camp near Munich, I
met with a man who survived the Holocaust and
who has taken on a life mission of announcing to
the world that God's love is deeper than the
sloughs of human depravity. He helped me understand how Corrie ten Boom's hopeful view of life
was even possible in such a place.

The man, Christian Reger, spent four years
as a prisoner in Dachau. His crime? He had
belonged to the Confessing Church, the branch of
the German state church which, under the leader-
ship of Martin Niemoller and Dietrich Bonhoeffer,
opposed Hitler. Reger, turned over to the authori-
ties by his church organist, was arrested and
shipped hundreds of miles away to Dachau.

Since liberation, Reger and other members of
the International Dachau Committee have worked
hard to restore the concentration camp as a lasting
monument and lesson to all humanity. "Never
Again" is their slogan. Nonetheless, the camp is
difficult to find, since the locals are understandably
reluctant to call attention to it.

The day I visited Dachau was gray, chilly,
and overcast. Morning fog hung low, close to the
ground, and as I walked droplets of moisture gathered on my face and hands. Thirty barracks once
stood on the site, and concrete foundation blocks a
foot high mark out their location. One has been

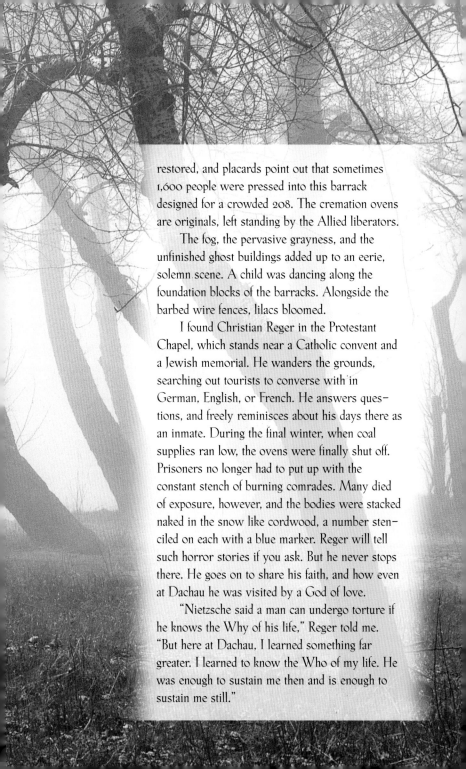

restored, and placards point out that sometimes 1,600 people were pressed into this barrack designed for a crowded 208. The cremation ovens are originals, left standing by the Allied liberators.

The fog, the pervasive grayness, and the unfinished ghost buildings added up to an eerie, solemn scene. A child was dancing along the foundation blocks of the barracks. Alongside the barbed wire fences, lilacs bloomed.

I found Christian Reger in the Protestant Chapel, which stands near a Catholic convent and a Jewish memorial. He wanders the grounds, searching out tourists to converse with in German, English, or French. He answers questions, and freely reminisces about his days there as an inmate. During the final winter, when coal supplies ran low, the ovens were finally shut off. Prisoners no longer had to put up with the constant stench of burning comrades. Many died of exposure, however, and the bodies were stacked naked in the snow like cordwood, a number stenciled on each with a blue marker. Reger will tell such horror stories if you ask. But he never stops there. He goes on to share his faith, and how even at Dachau he was visited by a God of love.

"Nietzsche said a man can undergo torture if he knows the Why of his life," Reger told me. "But here at Dachau, I learned something far greater. I learned to know the Who of my life. He was enough to sustain me then and is enough to sustain me still."

YOU DESERVE A BREAK TODAY

Patsy Clairmont

I'M AFRAID my husband took this thought, "Gimme a break," a little too literally. Last week he fell in our kitchen and suffered a triple fracture to his ankle. Now he is in a cast, on crutches, and is definitely taking a break as well as having one. Whereas I, who thought I was going to take a break from a busy year of travel and speaking, find myself galloping around our premises caring for my beloved . . . hand and, yep, foot.

Now don't get me wrong; I'm grateful to be Les's nurse. I wouldn't want to be anywhere but with him. It's just that life takes so many unexpected twists and turns right in the middle of some of our best-laid plans. We had moved two weeks before Les's fall, and we both had high expectations of how we would settle into our new abode. Now our teamwork has turned into me-work. To tell the truth, I'm not that handy.

I think the first sign that we were in for some interesting days, with Les laid up and me at the helm, was minutes after his fall. Our friend Dan was coming to assist our son Marty in maneuvering my injured husband to the car. Marty suggested I turn on the porch light for Dan's arrival. I dashed to the front door, and instead of turning on the light, I rang the doorbell. No, I can't tell you why I did that. Panicked? Possibly. Menopausal? Definitely. Space cadet? Precisely.

Since Les broke his right ankle, I have become the designated driver. Oh, boy, Les has been waiting for this chance—payback time for years of my advising him how to drive. Before I even got out of our yard for our first visit to the doctor, I came under Les's tutelage. Our new home has a rather long driveway that I have to back out of, and I'm not a back-up kind of woman. I'm more your full-speed-ahead kind of gal. My car's backseat window ledge is designed too high for me to see to back up, so I have to rely on my side mirrors. For some reason I can't stay on a straight-mirrored course, and we looked like a Weeble. (You know, those round-bottomed toys children have that wobble all over.) I was in the flower beds, then off the other side brushing the tree trunks, and then back over to the grass and onto the sidewalk before finally reaching the road. Les was amazed. Well, amazed might be understating his response. I watched as concern spread across his face (like hives). He seemed to realize he had several months of these yard exits to live through—and so does the yard.

Not only am I not great at backing up, but I'm also not that impressive at climbing up. Yet up is where I needed to go to pound the nails in the brackets to hold the curtains in the living room. Les looked pale as he observed me ascending the ladder. I assured him I could handle this task. But when I attempted to pound the itsy–bitsy nail into the wood, I dropped the bracket. I scampered down, scaled back up, and promptly dropped the hammer. Down the ladder I scurried again, grabbed the hammer, and made my way back up to the ceiling . . . huffing and puffing. (This was more aerobic than a StairMaster.) After the third drop (this time it was the nail), Les's head also dropped as he slowly shook it back and forth. Okay, okay, Bob Vila I'm not.

Although I did try a Vila–approach in our bathroom. I wanted to hang a cupboard that was heavy, and Les said I would have to nail it into the studs. One night I began to thump on the wall trying to detect the sound difference between wallboard and wood (as if I would know). Les heard my Morse code taps and jogged in on his crutches to prevent me from inadvertently ripping out a wall with my cupboard. O ye of little faith. Les then sent me to the store to buy a stud finder so we could "do it right." I made my way to the hardware department but couldn't locate the stud finders. Two men were working in that department, but I was hesitant to ask them because I was concerned they would think I was being fresh. Finally I blurted out, "Where are your stud finders?" They smiled. They knew where they were, but they couldn't figure out how they worked or what size batteries they needed. (That made me feel a lot better.)

Then I had them direct me to the toggle screws. I needed one, only one, to mount the toilet–paper holder. Uncertain which of the three thousand screws was correct, I purchased thirty–five of them to improve my odds of

"doing it right." Yep, you guessed it: they were all wrong.

C'mon, folks, gimme a break. I'm the one with a loose screw if I think I can do all these unnatural tasks. (Although I now know how to identify a stud finder and what kind of batteries it takes. I can even operate the thing.) I'm doing better backing the car out of the driveway, and with the exception of our glider, a tree, and several flowers, I've hardly rammed into anything. I've also learned when I need to put up curtain brackets to call Bob Vila. And when I need a break, even in the midst of twists and turns, to call upon the Lord.

LOOKING TO JESUS
Dave and Jan Dravecky

I MET TERRY SEVERAL YEARS AGO. She was an avid baseball fan and especially loved the San Francisco Giants. She lived in the Bay area and had followed my career and illness with great interest—not only because she adored the Grand Old Game, but because she was battling a terminal case of cancer.

I got her on the phone one day to encourage her in the deadly struggle she faced. We talked about our mutual interests and the excitement of major league baseball, as well as the highs and lows of being a Giants fan. In the middle of our conversation the course of our discussion suddenly changed, and we began talking about her difficult battle against cancer. I don't recall much of what I said, but I remember vividly what she told me. "The one thing that gets me through this as I lie here in my hospital bed," she declared, "is knowing every morning that, if God once more allows me to open my eyes, the first thing I'll see is a picture of Jesus hanging on the wall at the foot of my bed. When I see the picture of Jesus, somehow I get the strength to make it through another day." For someone who knows that, there's not a whole lot more that can be said. Terry discovered in her pain what all of us should remember every day of our lives: The way to get through the trials and difficulties of life is by looking to Jesus.

THE RAISIN MAKER

Barbara Johnson

RECENTLY I SPOKE AT THE RAISIN FESTIVAL in Dinuab, California, the Raisin Capital of the World. I learned a lot about raisins there and watched how they turn grapes into raisins that are juicy and sweet.

These raisin professionals use a unique process unlike anything I'd imagined. First, they take only the best California grapes. Then they give them the "spa treatment": the grapes are bathed in hot water followed by twenty-four hours of controlled dehydration in warm air. Finally, the raisins are cooled and gently washed again in warm water before being bundled in convenient packages. The process entails great care heating the initial hot-water bath, gradually cooling the water, then heating it again to insure plump, moist raisins. Other packers, they told us, dry the grapes in the sun, with questionable results.

I'm like a grape. When I'm left in the sun to dry, I lose my resilience, too. I end up washed-out with questionable nourishing qualities. Let's face it: We all get parched in the deserts of life. We need springs and pools to refresh us, to make us plump with faith and moist with good deeds.

Someone once said, "Christians are like tea. Their strength comes out in hot water." I say, "Christians are like grapes, too. In hot water, we get sweeter and juicier and prove that we can endure the process of life."

I don't know about you, but I sure don't want to end up an old pious prune. Nor do I want to end up like one of those hard little crusty raisins I sometimes find at the bottom of a box. I'll gladly take the hot water God puts me in because I know he knows I need it. Sometimes a good soaking brings out stuff I didn't know I had in me, like courage, dignity, compassion.

As for the controlled dehydration, I figure that's pretty much like God's love and patience. Twenty-four hours a day he's there, backing me up, guiding me forward, ready to speak, ready to listen. Never giving me more than I can bear. Always giving me just enough to make me sweeter than I was the day before.

Like the raisin producers, God knows we need cooling, too. Sometimes he cools our heels. There are times when love walks out the door and he

doesn't stop it from going. Maybe a friend moves out of town and he lets her leave. A job ends. A child rebels. The pages of the Bible stare at us blankly. He lets our passions cool off—even the spiritual ones. Even the seemingly good ones, the ones we thought were from him and would last forever. Only he knows why. But he's perfecting his raisins.

Just in time, he heats up the process again. Someone touches us with an encouraging word of kindness. A stranger gives us a warm smile. We share sympathetic warm tears or hear echoes of warm-hearted laughter when we least expect it. Maybe someone makes us chuckle in spite of ourselves or even at ourselves. God doesn't leave us cold, isolated, abandoned. He doesn't let us cool one minute too long.

I don't know about you, but I intend to cooperate with God in his work as Master Raisin Maker. I've tasted of the Lord's fruit, and it is good. Sweeter than honey. Ready to serve. And that's what I intend to do: serve him and others. I'm raisin' my prayers and praise to his beautiful will.

TREASURE IN THE TRASH
Luci Swindoll

TAX TIME IS USUALLY A DRAG for most of us. But there are some years when, after April 15, we feel absolutely poverty-stricken. That's how I felt some years ago when my taxes were so high I had little left for the "frivolous" things of life: little luxuries like buying books, taking trips, eating out.

I put myself on a very strict budget for three months, making it a point to write down every cent I spent for even the most insignificant things, like toothpaste or a Coke. I canceled various magazines and newspapers to which I had subscriptions and thought of every way under the sun to cut costs around my house. Actually, if the truth be known, it was kinda fun.

About three weeks into this exacting self-imposed regimen I was praying one afternoon that God would give me a creative idea of how I could have a lot of fun on little money. As I was leaving the home of a friend that evening I noticed she was tossing out a mum plant simply because its blooms were wilting. I felt sorry for the plant and asked her if I could have it. Incredulously, she announced, "But it's dead." I assured her that given enough time, I could revive it. She doubted that . . . which was the only challenge I needed to go full tilt on a new project. This was the answer to my prayer. I was going to create a garden, and it wasn't going to cost me a penny.

I was living in a complex where people would often toss their old dead (or dying) house plants in the garbage bins, with no further thought. I began to collect everybody's discarded mum plants. Some had been cut back, but most were just lying there with brown leaves, looking like there was no life left in them. In the course of the next three or four days I must have brought home more than twenty plants in various throes of death rattle, and nursed them back to health.

First, I cut them all back, watered them, and placed them on the upper deck just outside my bedroom window. I sang to them and played Mozart for them. When necessary, I killed aphids with a concoction of rubbing

alcohol, Murphy's Oil Soap, and water. I had become
Martha Stewart. My friends accused me of making my
own dirt.

I fertilized those precious little plants faithfully. In short,
I loved them into blooming again. And did they bloom! I
started taking pictures of them at various stages of growth:
with small buds, buds just breaking into blossoms, fully
blooming, and finally dying back. At one point, I'll bet I
counted seven or eight hundred blooms. Magnificent hues of
every color of mum in the world: yellow, orange, white,
purple, rust, brown, mauve . . . they were gorgeous! And
when people walked by or went outside, they looked up at
that array of color. Some pointed, others took pictures, and
everybody commented about my flower garden.

My friends who had teased me unmercifully about
collecting dead plants began asking for their plants back.
They begged me for mums. "Please, Luci, just enough for the
table for my dinner party?" No way! Every time I looked at
those sweet flowers I was reminded of God's brilliant
answer to my prayer.

Have you been down in the mouth lately? Want to do
something fun or uplifting for your spirit, but find yourself
with no money to splurge? Ask God for a creative idea. He
will give you one, and you will experience a dimension of
his giving that is different from the rest. It will be restorative
to your soul, because it will once again prove his ability to
provide for you, even in odd, zany, off–the–wall ways.

Excuse me . . . I'd like to sit here and chat longer, but
it's garbage day so I think I'll go see if I can find a few
dead plants.

A SONG IN HER HEART

Thelma Wells

OUR FAMILY ENJOYS good gospel music. We have discovered that praising God in song lifts our spirits, clears our heads, and opens a place for the Holy Spirit to speak to us.

Alaya, my one-and-a-half-year-old granddaughter, is always singing. From the moment she could utter sounds, she made music. When her mother, Lesa, secured newborn Alaya in her car seat, this child would make sounds. As she developed, those sounds were easily recognizable as tunes such as the ABC song, "Jesus Loves Me," "Row, Row, Row Your Boat," and "Jesus Loves the Little Children."

Alaya sings when she is eating, having her diaper changed, playing, standing, pulling up, watching television, bouncing in her swing, sitting in a car, attending church. Everywhere, all the time, she has a song in her heart.

At first I wondered how she kept the sweetness, calmness, contentment, and joyfulness of singing all the time. But as I thought about it, I decided Alaya has loving parents whom she can depend on to take care of her, comfortable and safe surroundings to live in, little responsibility, a love of singing, lots of attention when she sings, and joy because in her little heart she feels God's love.

Just as Alaya feels secure and loved, God offers the same to his children. He extends care to us by meeting our every need (Philippians 4:19) and comforting us when we go through trials (Psalm 23:4). He tells us to put our cares on him because he is responsible for our existence and future (1 Peter 5:6–7), stands ready to reveal to us truths about his Word (2 Timothy 2:15), and loves us so much he sacrificed his Son to save us (John 3:16).

Realizing all this, don't you think we have something to sing about? When you're going through your daily routine or when you face trials and tribulations, do you allow music to comfort you? When times are good, do you stop to sing for joy?

God enjoys the song we lift up in praise to him. He even reciprocates by singing back to us, as the verse in Zephaniah tells us, "He will rejoice

over you with singing."

Just think when we sing praises down here on earth, angels are singing around God's throne twenty-four hours a day, seven days a week: "Holy, holy, holy, Lord God Almighty, the earth is full of your glory." And we'll be joining them. An old Negro spiritual says, "If you miss me from singing down here and you can't find me nowhere, come on up to bright glory. I'll be singing up there."

Want to lift your spirits from the hustle and bustle of the day? Sing to the Lord. When praises go up, blessings come down. Now, isn't that something to sing about?

Master of music and all good things, I adore you. You create a melody of sweet singing in the hearts of those who love you. Even if we can't sing melodiously, we can sing for joy at the works of your hands. We can praise you in the morning, afternoon, evening, and the midnight hour. And you sing back to us. What a promise! Thank you that melodies linger on in our hearts long after our voices have given way. We appreciate that it's not the sound of our voices that moves you but the condition of our hearts. Amen

BITTER OR BETTER?
Charles Stanley

ONE DAY SEVERAL YEARS AGO, a phrase kept coming to my mind as I was praying: "The purifying work of pain." I didn't understand what that phrase meant, but I knew God had planted that phrase in my mind and that it was important. About two weeks later, my mother had a stroke, and over the next three months, I watched her die. I thought this was the pain that God had foretold. The loss of my mother was intensely painful for me, but throughout her suffering, God assured me that he was doing a purifying work in her—and in me. A refining process was going on in our lives.

Little did I know that the pain would not end when my mother died. One situation after the next followed until it seems that the hallmark of the last four years in my life has been pain. Yet, when I look back on those months and years, I truly can say, "I know God has purified me in many ways." God has shown me things about myself and has taught me things that have made me a much stronger, wiser, and better person than I was four years ago. He is turning things for good.

I can look back and see how God has softened me up, changed my thinking, expanded my compassion for others who are in pain. I wouldn't trade those changes for anything. What may appear to others from the outside to be devastating, appears to me to be providential. Painful experiences that occur in our lives should not be classified as curses. They have the potential to be the means toward blessing, and we are wise to regard them thus.

This doesn't mean that I understand all that has happened. Some things we may not fully understand until eternity. This doesn't mean that I hurt less. But a perspective that God is at work keeps me from anger, bitterness, and hostility. I have taken the approach, "I'm going to grow from this. I choose to be better, not bitter."

FINDING PEACE
Charles Colson

NO ONE WAS SURPRISED when Patti Awan stood during the informal praise time at the Sunday evening service. A young Sunday school teacher with an air of quiet maturity, she had given birth to a healthy son a few months earlier, a first child for her and her husband Javy. The congregation settled back for a report of the baby's progress and his parents' thanksgiving. They were totally unprepared for what followed.

Hanging onto the podium before her, Patti began. "Four years ago this week, a young girl sat crying on the floor of a New Jersey apartment, devastated by the news of a lab report. Unmarried and alone, she had just learned she was pregnant."

The congregation grew completely quiet; Patti's tear-choked voice indicated just who that young woman was.

"I considered myself a Christian at the time," she continued, "but had found out about Christ while in the drug scene. After I learned about Him, I knew I wanted to commit myself to Him, but I couldn't give up my old friends or my old habits. So I was drifting between two worlds—in one still smoking dope every day and sleeping with the man who lived in the apartment below mine; in the other, going to church, witnessing to others, and working with the church youth group.

"But being pregnant ripped through the hypocrisy of my double life. I had been meaning to get right with God, but I kept slipping back. Now I couldn't live a nice, clean Christian life like all those church people.

"I felt the only answer was to wipe the slate clean. I would get an abortion; no one in the church would ever know.

"The clinic scheduled an abortion date. I was terrified, but my boyfriend was adamant. My sister was furious with me for being so stupid as to get pregnant. Finally, in desperation I wrote my parents. They were staunch Catholics, and I knew they would support me if I

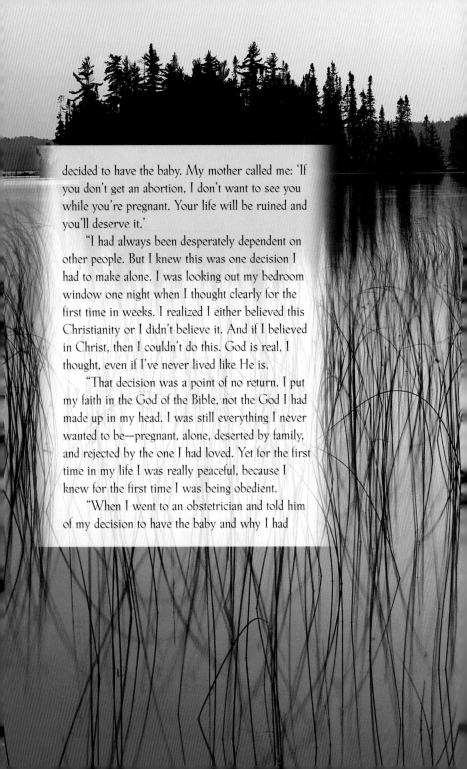

decided to have the baby. My mother called me: 'If you don't get an abortion, I don't want to see you while you're pregnant. Your life will be ruined and you'll deserve it.'

"I had always been desperately dependent on other people. But I knew this was one decision I had to make alone. I was looking out my bedroom window one night when I thought clearly for the first time in weeks. I realized I either believed this Christianity or I didn't believe it. And if I believed in Christ, then I couldn't do this. God is real, I thought, even if I've never lived like He is.

"That decision was a point of no return. I put my faith in the God of the Bible, not the God I had made up in my head. I was still everything I never wanted to be—pregnant, alone, deserted by family, and rejected by the one I had loved. Yet for the first time in my life I was really peaceful, because I knew for the first time I was being obedient.

"When I went to an obstetrician and told him of my decision to have the baby and why I had

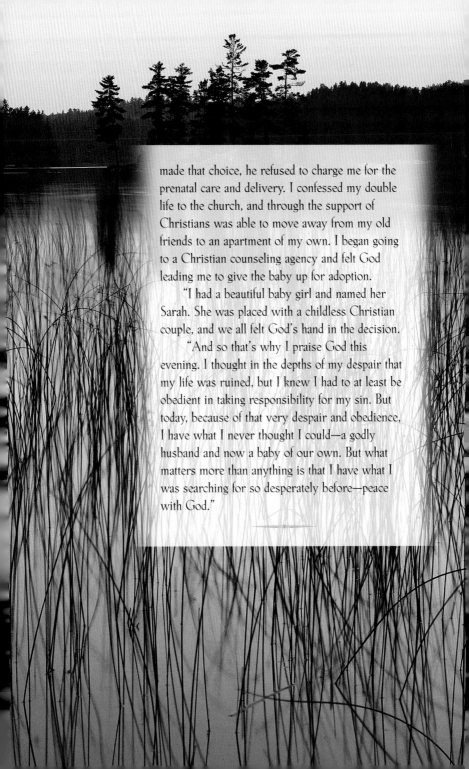

made that choice, he refused to charge me for the prenatal care and delivery. I confessed my double life to the church, and through the support of Christians was able to move away from my old friends to an apartment of my own. I began going to a Christian counseling agency and felt God leading me to give the baby up for adoption.

"I had a beautiful baby girl and named her Sarah. She was placed with a childless Christian couple, and we all felt God's hand in the decision.

"And so that's why I praise God this evening. I thought in the depths of my despair that my life was ruined, but I knew I had to at least be obedient in taking responsibility for my sin. But today, because of that very despair and obedience, I have what I never thought I could—a godly husband and now a baby of our own. But what matters more than anything is that I have what I was searching for so desperately before—peace with God."

LIFE IS FRAGILE

Luci Swindoll

DURING THE THIRTY YEARS I worked for Mobil Oil Corporation, hitting the freeway before dawn and dragging home after dark, I can tell you there were times I would have given anything for "the quiet life," whatever it took. I used to dream of retirement with its golf games, its manicures and pedicures, its ease and victory over the tyranny of racing to and from work. Longing for the good life, I would drive along as various cars cut in front of me, lickety split, threatening my spiritual and mental equilibrium, not to mention the hood ornament that almost became a part of another guy's trunk.

"Lord, get me outta here!" I would scream under my breath in my most sacerdotal tone. (Look up sacerdotal, it's a great word!)

One morning I was in my usual snit-fit to get to work when a young man on a motorcycle raced by on my right and passed through another lane of traffic on his left. Bad move! He was going way too fast to be weaving in and out of cars that way, and everyone was giving him a piece of their mind as he zipped by. My personal loving thoughts were, That idiot . . . he's not going to make it to the next exit if he keeps that up.

I drove another hundred yards or so, and then the traffic really began to crawl. Now what? As I inched forward I began to see the metal pieces of a broken motorcycle on the shoulder of the freeway. Then I spotted the body of someone covered with a sheet. Same motorcycle. Same boy. Somewhere between where I had been and where I was now, this guy died.

Needless to say, I was sobered and thought about little else that entire day. Even now, more than a decade later, I can still see that scene in my mind's eye. It gives me pause, partly because of the final tragedy of it all and partly because I know there are people out on that very freeway this minute, racing along just as I was . . . just as he was . . . oblivious to the fact that life is fragile. The freeway is the last place we think of slowing down or savoring our present moment. We simply want to get the driving over with, so we tear along with all our gripes and derring-do and madness, sometimes risking our very lives.

Even now, a number of years removed from the life I lived in the fast

lane, I sometimes forget that life is fragile. The fact that I have more time to dream my dreams and take my ease is no reason at all to disregard the moment I'm in by preferring to be somewhere else. I have to remind myself that wherever I am . . . fast lane or slow lane, in traffic or out of traffic, racing or resting . . . God is there. He is in me, abiding in me, thus making it possible for me to be all there myself.

Every day of our lives we make choices about how we're going to live that day. Wherever we find ourselves in this fragile existence we need to be reminded that life can be brighter than noonday and darkness like morning because we are living fully in this moment, secure in our hope in the Lord.

FAMILY MAN
Dave Dravecky

JAN AND I HAVE A DEAR FRIEND named Leslie Andrews, who lost her husband, Jim, to cancer. Leslie told us how her brother, Jeff, always put her husband on a pedestal. He looked up to Jim and said to him many times over the years, "I try so hard to be like you." They had very different personalities, but Jeff kept saying, "When I think of what I want to be, I want to be like you—but I can't quite pull it off."

Just hours after Jim died, a letter from Jeff arrived at the house. That letter read, "Jim, I finally realized that you weren't acting. The things you did came out of your relationship with Jesus Christ. It wasn't that you got up every day and said, 'Okay, I'm going to be really nice to Leslie today. I'm going to be really nice to my kids today; I'm not going to yell.' I finally get it. That is who you are because Jesus Christ is your Lord."

Jeff finally got it. He finally realized that he couldn't be a godly man merely by trying to imitate all the things he saw another godly man do. It wasn't Jim doing all those things anyway. It was Christ living in Jim and Jim responding to the Holy Spirit out of the love he had for God.

So what's the main lesson all of us can learn from Jim? Stay close to Jesus! Then, when we simply act like ourselves, we will reflect Jesus' love to the world.

HE DIDN'T DESERVE IT

Marilyn Meberg

OUR FIRST HOME was one that pleased Ken and me enormously. We loved our little fenced-in backyard and felt confident about the safety of both Jeff and Beth as they trundled about in it, often without need of our direct supervision.

On either side of the walkway leading to the front door was an area of decorative small rocks. Jeff loved to play in there with his Tonka trucks, creating roads and garages for his fleet of vehicles. Ken had attempted to impress upon Jeff's four-year-old mind the importance of keeping the rocks out of the grass because of the damage it could do to his lawnmower. In fact, Ken explained to Jeff that he was solely responsible for keeping the grass clear of rocks even if it were his friends and not Jeff who, in a burst of driving frenzy, managed to spew rocks into the grass.

One Friday morning as Jeff and I were bringing groceries into the house I noticed some rocks were strewn about the grass area near the front door. I suggested to Jeff that he would need to get out there and remove them since Daddy would be mowing the next day. Jeff was indignant at the suggestion. "I didn't get those rocks in there . . . Nell did!"

"It doesn't matter who got them there, sweetheart. It's your job to keep the grass clear. That's Daddy's deal with you."

"That's not right . . . I didn't do it." "I'm sorry, Jeff, but you still need to clear the grass whether it feels fair to you or not."

Jeff was always a mild-mannered little fellow and not the least prone to fits and fights. He trudged resolutely outside but from his body language I could see he was laboring under a burden of victimization.

The kitchen window was open and I could hear him

muttering to himself as he sifted through the grass removing rocks. I was enormously curious to know the contents of his muttering so I leaned in the direction of the window. "I'm just like Jesus . . . I'm just like Jesus . . . I'm just like Jesus."

That was the last thing I expected to hear. What in the world was going on in his little mind? I decided to go outside and help him with the rock detail and while there, ask him if he would talk about how he was just like Jesus. At first he would neither mutter nor talk to me. Finally, with my prodding, he retorted, "Well, Jesus never did anything bad and he got punished. That's just the same as me!"

I enveloped his troubled little face with my eyes and then swooped him into my arms. He didn't cry but I did.

Jeff's theology was a bit off, but we didn't go into it then. It is true that Jesus "who knew no sin" died that I, born in sin, might have eternal life. That is a difficult truth to comprehend at times. I love the clarity with which The Living Bible expresses this in Romans 5:15–17: "For this one man, Adam, brought death to many through his sin. But this one man, Jesus Christ, brought forgiveness to many through God's mercy. Adam's one sin brought the penalty of death to many, while Christ freely takes away many sins and gives glorious life instead. The sin of this one man, Adam, caused death to be king over all, but all who will take God's gift of forgiveness and acquittal are kings of life because of this one man, Jesus Christ."

Some years later, these regenerating truths became more clear to Jeff. Ultimately he came to understand that we not only identify with the sufferings of Christ, but we are set free because of the sufferings of Christ. What colossal good news!

HEART FOR THE LORD
Bill Hybels and Rob Wilkins

ANGIE GARBER, nearing the age of eighty, is a woman with many stories. The daughter of an Iowa farmer, she stayed at home to take care of her mentally unstable mother until late in her life. Instead of going to college, she says, she got polio. She has never been married. At the age of thirty-eight, while attending a seminary in Indiana, she was asked to teach at a mission on an Indian reservation in New Mexico. Because she had nothing else to do, and she had read James Fenimore Cooper as a child, she decided to go.

For more than four decades, she has lived in a tiny off-white home with three rooms: a combination kitchen and living room (not big enough for a couch), a bedroom just barely big enough for a single bed, and a bathroom. She has a Norge deluxe refrigerator that sounds like a small Piper Cub.

She has her luxuries, she says. A small organ to play hymns, a portable AM-FM radio with a cracked speaker to hear J. Vernon McGee and, in her front yard, a small cement pond with goldfish. In honor of forty years of service at the reservation, she was just recently given a television, the first she has owned.

Her focus in life has never been on things. "I don't want to just have things," she says, "When you love things, you use people. I don't care about getting things for my house. I've got enough, more than enough. The Bible says with food and raiment be satisfied." And, she adds with a laugh, a little gas for her pickup truck thrown in on the side. . . .

In such an environment, Angie has learned that personal value and purpose must flow exclusively from a relationship with Jesus Christ. "You have to keep your eyes on the Lord, you just can't start looking around. Your joy has to come from the Lord. The issue is not how many people come to know the Lord or not; the main thing is: Is your heart for the Lord? If you didn't love the Lord, you couldn't work or serve here."

UNCLE BROTHER
Thelma Wells

ONE OF THE MOST COLORFUL PEOPLE in my family is Uncle Lawrence Morris, Jr., my mother's only brother. His nickname is Uncle Brother. At more than seventy years old, he tries to act and think like a springtime chicken. He's always talking about his girlfriend, but I don't think he really has one. At least no one in the family has seen any sign of her!

Sixteen years ago, I became Uncle Brother's legal guardian because he was termed a "chronic alcoholic." Although he had accepted Christ as a young man, Uncle Brother had lived like the devil. He admits he has had his share of booze and all that goes with it. When he reached the point all he wanted was his drinking, someone had to care for him, and that someone turned out to be me. As his guardian, I made decisions he didn't agree with, but we couldn't deal with each other on level ground as one adult to another. It was a dark night in our relationship, and we didn't know if the morning would ever dawn.

But even when I was angry with him for the way he treated everyone, I prayed for him to return to the Lord. I prayed for the Holy Spirit to convict him and to give him no rest until he repented and started to live for God. I didn't want Uncle Brother to die without realizing he could enjoy a better life than the one he had chosen. He knew I loved him because I put up with him. And I often told him I loved him in spite of the way he responded to me when I said it.

Thanks be to God, we made it through that night; our sorrow turned to joy. For the past several years, Uncle Brother has made some major changes. Now he talks about how God has brought him through dangers seen and unseen. He praises God in song. He watches Christian television. He reads his Bible. He bridles his tongue. He speaks affectionately about people. He has changed his friends. He is respected in his community. He is concerned about other family members. He attends family celebrations. He's fun to be around. His mourning has turned to gladness and so has everyone else's in the family.

With my uncle, weeping endured for about ten years, but God was always present. He never left Uncle Brother alone. And he was waiting for my uncle to reopen his heart.

We endured turbulence and turmoil as the norm for years. But today, my uncle can sing with me, "This joy we have, the world didn't give it and the world can't take it away!" Are you dealing with someone whom you feel will never change? Do you vacillate between wishing he would change and just wanting him to leave you alone? Have you given up expecting good things from that person?

Nobody is so far from God that he can't get back to the Lord. Our responsibility is to keep knocking at God's door about that person, to keep believing God will answer our prayers. Thank God for what he will do. Patiently but expectantly wait on the Lord. Renew your hope!

Lord, that you never give up on us is more consoling than I can express. Just to watch you move people from the pits of hell to the portholes of glory is over- whelming. Let me always remember that because you made us you can change us. Increase my patience with those who seem like hopeless causes. And renew my persistence in praying for them. Amen.

SCRIPTURES THAT CAUSE US TO LOOK UP

As for me, I will always have hope;
I will praise you more and more,
O Lord.

Psalm 71:14

Remember your word to your servant,
O LORD, for you have given me hope.

Psalm 119:49

Why are you downcast, O my soul?
Why so disturbed within me? Put
your hope in God, for I will yet praise
him, my Savior and my God.

Psalm 42:11

The LORD is good to those whose
hope is in him, to the one who seeks
him; it is good to wait quietly for the
salvation of the LORD.

Lamentations 3:25–26

May the God of hope fill you with all
joy and peace as you trust in him, so
that you may overflow with hope by
the power of the Holy Spirit.

Romans 15:13

Praise be to the LORD, to God our
Savior, who daily bears our burdens.

Psalm 68:19

"Have faith in God," Jesus said.

Mark 11:22

Guide me in your truth and teach me,
for you are God my Savior, and my
hope is in you all day long.

Psalm 25:5

May our Lord Jesus Christ himself
and God our Father, who loved us and
by his grace gave us eternal encouragement and good hope, encourage
your hearts and strengthen you in
every good deed and word.

2 Thessalonians 2:16–17

Through Christ you believe in God,
who raised him from the dead and
glorified him, and so your faith and
hope are in God.

1 Peter 1:21

May integrity and uprightness protect
me, because my hope is in you, O
LORD.

Psalm 25:21

I wait for the LORD, my soul waits,
and in his word I put my hope.

Psalm 130:5

May your unfailing love rest upon
us, O LORD, even as we put our hope
in you.

Psalm 33:22

The LORD is my rock, my fortress and my deliverer; my God is my rock, in whom I take refuge. He is my shield and the horn of my salvation, my stronghold.

Psalm 18:2

For the eyes of the LORD range throughout the earth to strengthen those whose hearts are fully committed to him.

2 Chronicles 16:9

The LORD upholds all those who fall and lifts up all who are bowed down.

Psalm 145:14

Let everyone who is godly pray to you while you may be found, O God; surely when the mighty waters rise, they will not reach him.

Psalm 32:6

Jesus said, "Peace I leave with you; my peace I give you. I do not give to you as the world gives. Do not let your hearts be troubled and do not be afraid."

John 14:27

Now may the Lord of peace himself give you peace at all times and in every way. The Lord be with all of you.

2 Thessalonians 3:16

Jesus said, "Come to me, all you who are weary and burdened, and I will give you rest. Take my yoke upon you and learn from me, for I am gentle and humble in heart, and you will find rest for your souls."

Matthew 11:28–29

When I said, "My foot is slipping," your love, O LORD, supported me. When anxiety was great within me, your consolation brought joy to my soul.

Psalm 94:18–19

God has shown kindness by giving you rain from heaven and crops in their seasons; he provides you with plenty of food and fills your hearts with joy.

Acts 14:17

My soul finds rest in God alone; my salvation comes from him.

Psalm 62:1

This is what the Sovereign LORD, the Holy One of Israel, says: "In repentance and rest is your salvation, in quietness and trust is your strength."

Isaiah 30:15

Set your hope fully on the grace to be given you when Jesus Christ is revealed.

1 Peter 1:13

Be at rest once more, O my soul, for the LORD has been good to you.

Psalm 116:7

May the LORD answer you when you are in distress; may the name of the God of Jacob protect you.

Psalm 20:1

God is our refuge and strength, an ever-present help in trouble.

Psalm 46:1

God saves the needy from the clutches of the powerful. So the poor have hope.

Job 5:15–16

"Because he loves me," says the LORD, "I will rescue him; I will protect him, for he acknowledges my name. He will call upon me, and I will answer him; I will be with him in trouble, I will deliver him and honor him."

Psalm 91:14–15

We wait in hope for the LORD; he is our help and our shield.

Psalm 33:20

I am poor and needy; come quickly to me, O God. You are my help and my deliverer; O LORD, do not delay.

Psalm 70:5

God has delivered me from all my troubles, and my eyes have looked in triumph on my foes.

Psalm 54:7

O LORD, be not far off; O my Strength, come quickly to help me.

Psalm 22:19

Be merciful to me, O LORD, for I am in distress; my eyes grow weak with sorrow, my soul and my body with grief. My life is consumed by anguish and my years by groaning; my strength fails because of my affliction, and my bones grow weak.

Psalm 31:9–10

O LORD, do not forsake me; be not far from me, O my God. Come quickly to help me, O LORD my Savior.

Psalm 38:21–22

How priceless is your unfailing love, O LORD! Both high and low among men find refuge in the shadow of your wings.

Psalm 36:7

Give me a sign of your goodness, that my enemies may see it and be put to shame, for you, O LORD, have helped me and comforted me.

Psalm 86:17

"I have seen man's ways, but I will heal him; I will guide him and restore comfort to him, creating praise on the lips of the mourners in Israel. Peace, peace, to those far and near," says the LORD. "And I will heal them."

Isaiah 57:18–19

Praise be to the God and Father of our Lord Jesus Christ, the Father of compassion and the God of all comfort, who comforts us in all our troubles, so that we can comfort those in any trouble with the comfort we ourselves have received from God.

2 Corinthians 1:3–4

O my Comforter in sorrow, my heart is faint within me.

Jeremiah 8:18

My soul is weary with sorrow; strengthen me according to your word.

Psalm 119:28

Let the peace of Christ rule in your hearts, since as members of one body you were called to peace. And be thankful.

Colossians 3:15

I sought the LORD, and he answered me; he delivered me from all my fears.

Psalm 34:4

Cast all your anxiety on God because he cares for you.

1 Peter 5:7

The LORD makes me lie down in green pastures, he leads me beside quiet waters, he restores my soul.

Psalm 23:2–3

The LORD is my strength and my shield; my heart trusts in him, and I am helped. My heart leaps for joy and I will give thanks to him in song. The LORD is the strength of his people, a fortress of salvation for his anointed one.

Psalm 28:7–8

LOOK AHEAD

IF YOU HAVE EVER RUN IN A RACE, you probably know about "hitting the wall." It's not just that your feet, legs, and lungs hurt and that you feel drained of every bit of energy. It's that you have all of that pain with no end in sight. There's no finish line, no goal, no prize. So your mind whispers, "What's the use? . . . You'll never make it! . . . Give up." Every veteran runner will admit that the mental battles usually are much tougher than the physical ones.

Runners in life's race often "hit the wall" as well. Struggling with setbacks

and sorrows, despair begins to creep like fog around the edges of the mind, obscuring the finish. And you feel like giving in . . . giving up. That's when you need to look ahead to your goal. As Paul wrote, "But one thing I do: Forgetting what is behind and straining toward what is ahead, I press on toward the goal to win the prize for which God has called me heavenward in Christ Jesus" (Philippians 3:13–14).

God has a great future for you. In faith look ahead, trusting in his goodness and love. TAKE HOPE.

HE LEADETH ME

Joseph H. Gilmore & William B. Bradbury

He leadeth me! O blessed thought! O words with heavenly
    comfort fraught!
Whatever I do, wherever I be, Still 'tis God's hand that leadeth me.

He leadeth me, He leadeth me, By His own hand He leadeth me:
His faithful follower I would be, For by His hand He leadeth me.

Sometimes amid scenes of deepest gloom, Sometimes where Eden's
    bowers bloom,
By waters still, o'er troubled sea, Still 'tis His hand that leadeth me!

He leadeth me, He leadeth me, By His own hand He leadeth me:
His faithful follower I would be, For by His hand He leadeth me.

Lord, I would clasp Thy hand in mine, Nor ever murmur nor repine,
Content, whatever lot I see, Since 'tis my God that leadeth me!

He leadeth me, He leadeth me, By His own hand He leadeth me:
His faithful follower I would be, For by His hand He leadeth me.

And when my task on earth is done, When, by Thy grace, the
    victory's won,
Even death's cold wave I will not flee, Since God through Jordan
    leadeth me.

He leadeth me, He leadeth me, By His own hand He leadeth me:
His faithful follower I would be, For by His hand He leadeth me.

A FAITH SHELF

Dave Dravecky

IF YOU WALKED INTO MY OFFICE, you would probably notice the baseballs on my shelf. Each one commemorates a special achievement from my baseball career. There's the ball from my first win as a professional ballplayer in the minor leagues, when I played in Shelby, North Carolina. There's the ball from my first major league win when I was playing for the San Diego Padres: July 4, 1982. I pitched against the San Francisco Giants and the guy I beat was Atlee Hammaker (who later became my close friend). When I put that ball on my shelf, I did not know that exactly five years later, on July 4, 1987, I would be traded to the San Francisco Giants. I also have my 1983 autographed All-Star ball and my 1989 "Earthquake World Series" ball autographed by all the guys on our team.

Each one of those baseballs on my shelf are prized, but there are two that I prize more highly than the rest. The first is the ball from my best pitching performance in the major leagues, when I threw a one-hit shutout against the Los Angeles Dodgers. The other is the ball that I hit out of the park from my first home run in the major leagues. Again we were playing against the Dodgers. We were at Jack Murphy Stadium in San Diego in 1986, the count was three and two, and I was batting off a left-handed pitcher named Dennis Powell. Those achievements are indelibly etched into my memory.

Just because I could no longer play the game, I didn't take the baseballs off my shelf. I prize the memories and the accomplishments they represent. Looking at them helps me to remember that I have enjoyed great accomplishments in my work life. We all feel better about ourselves when we consider our work achievements. But you know what else encourages me? I didn't know what the future held when I pitched my first major league win against Atlee Hammaker. I had no way of knowing what a good friend Atlee would become to me. I had no way of knowing about the other balls that would one day be placed on my shelf alongside that first one.

I'm encouraged to know that there are shelves yet to be filled in my future, just as there are in yours. There are accomplishments waiting to be achieved and friendships waiting to be made. Maybe we should all put up an empty shelf, in faith that what we are dreaming of now will, one day, be achieved. God alone knows what could end up on our shelves!

ONE STEP AT A TIME

Patsy Clairmont

GENE IS A GENTLEMAN FARMER and has been the "boss" of many animals over the years, although it's true that animals have minds of their own. He learned that early on. When he was only eight, he earned the money for his first cow, Daisy, by selling potatoes. Daisy was a Hereford and in time presented her proud owner with two calves.

Gene went on a camping trip once, and during his absence, Daisy roamed off. For a week she traipsed about the countryside. When Gene returned and finally found his cow, she had contracted pinkeye. Because it had not been attended to immediately, Daisy lost her sight. Young Gene was heartsick. He loved his cow, and he was afraid they would have to put her down.

But because Daisy had been around the barn a few times, so to speak, she still knew how to find her way between the pasture and her bed. Gene watched in amazement as Daisy would near the barn, then step gingerly forward until her horns would touch the building. Then, pressing her horns lightly against the wood, she would trace her way around the barn to its opening and slip into her stall.

I love that story. No, not because I feel like an old cow, but because Daisy knew the path so well. I pray that I can follow in the Lord's footsteps so consistently that even when I can't "see," I'll continue to walk in his ways by faith. Why, even my old hard head, when bowed in his presence, can moo–ve me in the right direction. For when we graze in his pasture, we will rest in our beds—guaranteed.

JUST KEEP PEDALING

Barbara Johnson

WHEN I LEARNED TO RIDE a bicycle, I did it badly—at least in comparison to other neighborhood kids. I had no sense of balance. I'd wobble and roll, wibble and rock. I ended up with scraped knees and shins. It seemed no matter how much I wanted to, I couldn't get the two-wheeler to stay upright. I thought I'd be the only kid in second grade who couldn't ride a bike. Fortunately, a neighborhood friend offered to teach me how to ride. He seemed so confident. "It's simple," he said. "The problem is you haven't got enough momentum going to keep in balance. Once you get going fast enough long enough you won't have any trouble at all." "Uh, I don't think so," I answered. "Fast enough, long enough? I think I hear my mother calling me home." And I was outta there. But the next day, my friend was back. "Come on," he said. "I'll teach you how to ride today." He placed my hand on the handlebars of my red bicycle, a color that matched my emotion: deep fear. Trembling, I put my feet on the pedals while he held the bike steady. As we started to move forward he said, "When I let go, keep pedaling! Don't be afraid of the momentum. Use it!" Tromp, tromp, tromp. Faster. Faster. I could hear his feet pounding the pavement. He kept me upright, but we were going fast. He was huffing when he shoved the seat of my bike forward. I shot down the road like a miniature rocket. From far behind me he yelled, "Use the momentum!" In panic, I kept pedaling just like he told me to—and I've been pedaling ever since. In the kingdom of God, there are days we think we'll never learn our lesson because circumstances are too overwhelming. We view difficult circumstances as threats, not opportunities. We think they are going to hurt (and they might). We want to grow up and do exciting things like the other kingdom kids, but we don't want to bloody our knees and shins in the process. Then the Holy Spirit whispers, "Come on, I'll teach you. I'll show you how to use momentum to get where God wants you to go with your life." The Holy Spirit knows we have what it takes to keep upright once we're shoved ahead. Yes, there are lots of wobbles along the way and more than a few dangers. But with time we learn to assume control over those things—if we just keep pedaling.

LEAVING TOMORROW TO GOD

Barbara Johnson

RECENTLY, ON A VISIT to the North Carolina mountains, I encountered a sign on the winding highway that read, Limited Visibility Ahead. This is a rare sign in California, where freeway expanses give spacious views (except for traffic tie–ups, of course— oh, yeah, and smog). But the phrase, Limited Visibility, caused me to recall an old song entitled "If We Could See Beyond Today":

If we could see, if we could know, we often say,
but God in love a veil does throw across our way.
We cannot see what lies before, and so we cling to
*   Him the more.*
He leads us till this life is o'er, trust and obey.

The idea of God's throwing a veil across our way touches me, doesn't it you? How wonderful that we don't have to know the future but can be assured that a veil separates us from the up–ahead. We only have to concern ourselves with the problems and circum– stances of today, leaving tomorrow to him. A friend of mine owns a dog who has her own way of throwing a veil on the future. When it's time for a visit to the vet, the dog has to be boosted into the car's backseat, where she immediately plants herself looking out the back window. My friend isn't sure if this gesture is the dog's way of expressing anger at her owner, avoiding what's up ahead, or showing her disorientation at the dizzying thought of the car's destination. How many of us would turn our backs on the future if we could clearly see what it held? If I had known at age twenty-five that I would lose two sons and be estranged from a third, I think I would have immediately "resigned." But because our future is unknown, we just take a plateful of life at a time. After all, yesterday is a canceled check, and tomorrow is only a promissory note. But today is cash. We have the vision for today, not tomorrow with its uncertainties and challenges. I recall reading that "It is the weight of the tomorrows that drives men mad." Life isn't a destination but a journey, and so we all encounter unexpected curves, turning points, mountaintops, and valleys. We discover the best in ourselves as each event occurs and shapes us into who we are.

GOD WILL BE THERE
Charles Stanley

ASK YOURSELF squarely, "How much do you think God loves you?"

I asked one woman this question one day when she came to see me in the wake of her husband's death following a lengthy illness. She was angry with God and finally blurted out, "God abandoned me when I needed him the most."

I assured her that God never abandons us. He assures us always of his presence. I knew that the problem was not that God had abandoned her in her time of trial, but rather, that she had turned to everyone and everything other than God in her time of trial. She had abandoned him. Rather than confront her with this fact, however—which I knew she couldn't accept at that time—I asked her, "How much do you think God loves you?"

She said bitterly, "I don't think he loves me at all."

"I don't believe that's possible," I said. "That would make you the only exception in the history of the entire world."

She seemed stunned. I continued, "First John 4:8 tells us that God is love. Love is the foremost of his attributes. And whatever God has as an attribute, he has as an infinite, pure, and perfect attribute. God's nature doesn't change. If he loves one person, he loves all people."

"Then what happened?" she said. "Why did God let my husband get so sick and suffer so much and die? How could God love me and let that happen?" "I don't know," I said.

"I don't know why God acts as he acts, but I do know that God never stopped loving you, or your husband, for one moment. I suspect that you are angry at God right now because you are afraid that he won't be there to help you in the coming days."

She nodded silently as tears filled her eyes. "I want to assure you," I said, "that God will be there for you. I don't know all that God has for you in the future, but I do know this, he desires for you to trust him completely. He desires for you to rely upon him every step of the way, every day, all the way to heaven."

ALIVE INSIDE

Sheila Walsh

LET ME GIVE YOU A GLIMPSE into the dream—and the courage—of a young Siberian woman whom I know through my friend Marlene.

In her late teens Lida Vashchenko longed for freedom to be able to worship Christ freely. To make that freedom a reality, she walked through her fear, got on a train to Moscow, and pushed her way through the gates of the American embassy, seeking asylum. When no one knew what to do with her, she began a hunger strike. After thirty days, at eighty pounds, she was taken from the embassy to a hospital. Weak and hardly able to stand, she was forced to stand in front of sixteen men in her underwear as they questioned her.

"Do you think at eighty pounds you can fight the entire Soviet nation?" a KGB officer asked her.

"No," she replied, "but I serve a God who can."

After seven years living as a virtual prisoner, Lida came to the United States. When Marlene asked her what it was like to live under that kind of intimidation, Lida replied, "It is better to die doing something for God than to live doing nothing at all."

Perhaps you think that those words are more credible on a movie screen than from the lips of a young Siberian woman, but it really all depends on where you are standing in life. When you become alive inside, really alive to the edges of heaven that invade our world all the time, what is there to be afraid of? When you know deep in the marrow of your bones that this life that we cling to is a mere shadow of our real lives that are hidden, safe with God in heaven, there is a limit to what anyone can do to us. Hebrews 13:5–6 quotes two books of the Old Testament, adding a "confident" transition: " 'Never will I leave you; never will I forsake you.' So we say with confidence, 'The Lord is my helper; I will not be afraid. What can man do to me?' " Exactly!

TAKING THE RISK
Patsy Clairmont

MY HUSBAND LED A HIGH-RISK CHILDHOOD. He was wild and a risk-taker: you know, the type you pray doesn't move in next door. He was raised in Gay, Michigan (no, I didn't make that up). Les, his four brothers, and sister, Diane, lived in their small town (population one hundred) nine hundred yards from Lake Superior. In the winter they averaged two hundred inches of snow—although it wasn't unusual to have three and even four hundred inches in one season. We can only imagine the snow adventures that created.

One winter when Les was about ten years old, he and some friends were breaking snowdrifts off cliffs. They would walk out as close to the cliff's edge as they dared and then kick until the drift would break off and tumble to the ground twenty-five feet below. Once Les misjudged the edge and tumbled headlong to the ground below. The large accumulation of snow softened his landing, but the broken snowdrift followed Les. In seconds the only sign of him was two feet sticking out, and they were kicking. His friends scrambled to his rescue, digging him out with their hands. Now that's enough to leave a permanent set of chill bumps on a kid and on his mother (if she ever found out). Some risks aren't worth taking. Like bear tampering . . . One of Les's childhood diversions was to throw rocks at bears while they were dining at the dump. (Call me cautious, but I wouldn't have the starch to throw a rock at a bear if it was stuffed and mounted, much less if it was breathing.) When the bears became agitated, they would chase the kids up a hill until the children were out of sight. Believing they were rid of their tormentors, the bears would return to the dump only to have these daring imps reappear. One time Les was visiting his cousins, and they decided to stir up some bear fur—only these annoyed bears became ticked. The boys ran until their hearts were in their mouths and still the bears were in hot pursuit. All parties involved were thinking about the fellows becoming the third course of a seventeen course meal. But of course, since I'm married to Les, you can guess that he narrowly escaped, as did his cousins.

Les did decide that, after his brush with Smokey and the bandits, he

wouldn't bug any more bears. Some risks aren't worth taking. . . . That's the problem with risks: some are worth taking, some aren't. Some of the risks I've taken that turned out poorly have been the greatest teachers for making good future choices. And some sure-shot risks have been long-term detrimental. Hmm, this is complex. Bad could be good, good could be miserable, bad could be disabling, and good could turn out great. I guess that's why it's called a risk.

I'm really not one to dive headlong into life, but I don't want to miss the wave and be left high and dry on the shore. I wonder if that's how Peter felt when he stepped from the boat's safety to join Jesus in the raging sea (Matthew 14:28–32). Peter wanted to take the risk, but then he focused on the storm and began to sink. Stepping on the water wasn't risky for Peter because he was walking toward Jesus. No, the big risk was taking his eyes off the Lord and being overwhelmed by his circumstances. Even then the Lord extended a helping hand. That's the safety factor in facing life's risks: Jesus. If you are walking toward him to the best of your ability, he will see you through life's unpredictable waters—but you must risk launching the boat.

CALMING THE HEART

Luci Swindoll

A VERY DEAR FRIEND of mine who teaches
elementary school music got a timely reminder
recently of how much simpler life can be when
God is in the picture. One Monday afternoon
she was feeling apprehensive about having to
change the date for a musical program on the
school calendar. It meant she had to face the
principal, ask for the change, and possibly have
her request rejected. As you may know, one can't
just arbitrarily switch the dates of the orchestra
concert and the big basketball game, for example.
These events are determined months in advance
and are generally set in concrete!

As she busied herself in her classroom, she
rehearsed what she would say to the principal.
The fear began to rise in her so much that her
anxiety was out of proportion to her upcoming
request. She had that "fretful" feeling.

While dusting off her desk, she swept a
small scrap of paper to the floor. When she
picked it up, she was amazed to read the words,
"When I am afraid, I will trust in you." She
could hardly believe her eyes; it was just the
encouragement she needed to accomplish the task
at hand. She smiled to herself, took a deep breath,
and walked straight to the principal's office for
her talk. Everything worked out beautifully, and

the date was changed on the calendar with only minor adjustments. Several days later, a little girl in one of her music classes came up to her and whispered, "Mrs. Jacobs, have you by any chance seen a piece of paper with the words, 'When I am afraid, I will trust in you' written on it?" My friend told the child she had seen that paper and it was at her desk.

"Is it yours, Rachel?" The child told her it was. Wanting to make the most of the moment, my friend asked, "Are you all right, honey? How did you happen to have that piece of paper in the first place? Is there anything I can help you with?" Rachel confided, "Well, remember a few days ago when we had to take all those tests? I was afraid I couldn't pass, so my mom put that note in my lunch box that day, and it really helped me. Then somehow I lost it."

My friend then explained how the child's loss was her gain. She expressed that she too had feared something, found the paper on the floor, and was reminded to face and overcome that fear by trusting God. The very thing that had calmed the heart of the little child was the same thing that calmed the heart of the wise and mature schoolteacher.

SAFE IN HIS HANDS

Sheila Walsh

SINCE I'VE BECOME A MOTHER, the fear of loss of control has gone to a new depth: fearing for the well-being of my child. With the delight of motherhood came a vulnerability that I have never experienced before. And it hit me full-force just days after Christian's birth. What looked to me like a Bermuda tan the doctor said was jaundice. He explained that because the baby had arrived three weeks early, his liver was not quite ready. They took some blood and told us to take him out in the December California sunshine for as much of the day as possible. We were to bring Christian back to the doctor the next day; if the "billirubin levels" hadn't improved they would arrange for lights to be delivered to our home. I held him as they took blood from his tiny foot. He cried so hard it almost broke my heart.

We went home. Hours later the doctor called and told us to get Christian into pediatric intensive care within the hour, because something else had "shown up" in his blood. We threw a few things in the car, including the dog to drop off at the kennel, not knowing how long we would be at the hospital. Barry ran into the kennel with Bentley, leaving me alone with Christian and feeling absolutely desperate.

"Please don't do this!" I cried out loud to God, tears rolling down my face. "Please don't take my little boy." If someone had walked up to me at that point and said, "Sheila, will you relinquish your son to the Lord?" I would have said "No." I'm sorry Abraham. I was so afraid that if I said yes, God would take him.

In thirty minutes Barry and I were being told how to scrub up (for ten minutes!) and how to put masks and gowns on. We were escorted into intensive care, to unit D-5. It all seemed so clinical, but this was our tiny baby lying in that plastic incubator. When a nurse said they would need to tape a patch over his eyes, I gasped, "But he'll be afraid."

"No, he won't," she said kindly. "Remember, he's kind of familiar with the dark."

A doctor explained the problem—that Christian's white blood count

was off. "It's not leukemia," he said, "but there are other things we need to look for."

The next morning the doctor told us there had been a mistake and that apart from a little jaundice there had never been anything wrong with Christian. As we drove home with our baby boy, strong images were burned into my mind. The look on the faces of others parents in the unit, the tiny baby in the room next to Christian's who labored hard for every breath, the fear that grabbed my heart when an alarm went off over our incubator and the relief when the nurse told me it was from another room, my feelings of guilt that I was glad it was another baby. I'd never felt such primal emotions. I'd never felt so desperate, so afraid, so small, so out of control. How can such joy and terror come wrapped in the same gift? I wondered. As I tucked him into his blue bassinet by our bed, I said to him, "Okay, here are the ground rules. You can go out and play when you are twenty if you wear protective gear, and you may start dating when you're thirty-five!" His dad came and stood behind me laughing at my speech. Once more we placed Christian—as well as ourselves—in God's hands.

THAT'S THE DIFFERENCE
Joni Eareckson Tada

I'M AN ARTIST; I draw and paint. I write books for both children and adults. I've made a movie. I've recorded albums. I have a radio show and a ministry with Joni and Friends that lets me travel all over the world talking about Jesus. But these are not the things that make my mark in eternity. Jesus asks the same thing of me that he asks of you. We must both learn to trust and obey.

One hot July day, a lifetime ago, I dived into the cold, murky waters of the Chesapeake Bay. When they pulled me from the water, I was paralyzed. I thought my life was over. I thought I would never be happy again. I didn't see how God could possibly use my paralysis for good.

But God knew. Maybe his idea of good for me didn't mean getting back the use of my hands or legs. But His idea of good meant a big change in my attitude and in the way I look at what's important in life. God's idea of good also meant reaching out to others . . . the disabled people I met through Joni and Friends, and many others around the world.

Yes, there are times when it's still hard living in my wheelchair. But I'm always learning to put my life in His hands and my trust in Him. And that makes all the difference in the world!

FEELING STUCK
Sheila Walsh

WE PLACE OUR FAITH in a God who is faithful—even if and when we don't "get the plan."

Let me give you an illustration from my own life with baby Christian. Christian does not like his car seat. I wasn't prepared for this. My nephew, David, was comforted by his car seat more than anything else, and I thought all babies came that way. Apparently not. Some days Christian can be distracted by his plastic frog or by his biter bunny or by Barry and me singing "Jesus loves me, this I know" at the top of our lungs, but there are days when nothing helps and he wails like someone being tortured. He just doesn't get it. He wants to be held. I watched him in the rearview mirror the other day, and all of a sudden I saw myself in him. He was red-faced and cross. I couldn't explain to a six-month-old baby that the reason he was in a car seat was for his own good. I couldn't make him understand that it was because I loved him that he was strapped into this contraption. All he knew was that he wanted out, that his mother had the power to do it, and that she wouldn't.

I saw how I must seem to God so many times. I don't always understand what the Lord is doing in and through my life. I must seem to God to be a red-faced screaming little baby who thinks she knows best and actually doesn't have a clue. And yet as I watch him turn all the colors of the rainbow, I love him passionately. Just as I will never stop the car and toss Christian out, God in his faithfulness holds on to us when we "don't like the plan." "The Lord is faithful, and he will strengthen and protect you" (2 Thessalonians 3:3).

LIFE ON THE EDGE

by Lee Strobel

FOUR YEARS BEFORE I first talked with Yolanda Lugo, she had developed Hodgkin's disease, which is cancer of the lymph system. For a twenty-year-old woman just beginning to enjoy life, it was a devastating diagnosis, especially since physicians warned her that the disease was already spreading rather extensively through her body.

Yolanda told me how she had asked God to give her the strength to battle her illness, and he did. He gave her courage and fortitude as she underwent chemotherapy, radiation treatment, and surgery. Eventually her cancer went into remission.

Despite her suffering, Yolanda kept alive her dream of becoming a New York City police officer. She persevered because of her desire "to serve and protect," and finally, at age twenty-four, she was selected to join the department. It was a personal triumph for her—but she never foresaw how God would choose to use her illness to accomplish something that nobody else could have done.

The drama unfolded one day when Yolanda was driving home on the Verrazano Narrows Bridge, which connects Staten Island and Brooklyn. Suddenly a man jumped from his car and clambered to the top of a bridge abutment that was two hundred feet above the water.

Yolanda slammed on her brakes and ran over. "What are you doing?" she shouted.

"Get away from me!" came the reply. "I'm going to jump! I'm going to kill myself!"

Yolanda had never faced anything like this before. She wasn't sure what to do, so she just tried talking to him. He responded by cutting her off. "Look, get out of here!" he shouted. "I know you don't care about me!"

"Hey, I'm off duty. I didn't have to stop. I don't have to be here. I don't have to talk to you," Yolanda said. "But I want to. I want to help."

The man paused. "Well, then," he said. "Come on up."

Yolanda wasn't fond of heights, and this abutment overlooked a twenty-story drop to the icy water below. But she only hesitated for a moment. Then Yolanda—who weighed all of ninety-nine pounds—climbed up. When she managed to get close enough to the man, she tried to talk him down again, but every time, he would turn hostile and threaten once more to jump.

"You don't care about me!" he said. "Nobody does. My wife has left me; I've got all kinds of family problems. I'm going to end it all right now."

He was poised to leap. Yolanda had only a split second to respond. But when she spoke, her words stopped him cold. "I know about problems," she said softly.

The man was taken off guard. Again he paused. "What do you mean?" he asked, sounding genuinely curious. "How can a person like you know about problems?"

Yolanda told him, "I've got cancer."

"Really? Where do you have cancer?"

Yolanda started describing her illness to him. She talked about her own fears and uncertainties. She spoke about the pain she had endured. And she explained how God had helped her cope with her circumstances.

"I got help," she said. "Please—let me help you."

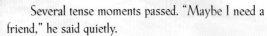

Several tense moments passed. "Maybe I need a friend," he said quietly.

Yolanda smiled. "Then I'll be your friend."

I don't know if any psychiatrist could have talked that desperate man out of suicide. He was right on the edge of leaping into oblivion. But I know this: he connected with Yolanda because of the pain and problems she had gone through. God used her own pain to reach that man in the unique way that he needed to be helped.

In the end he climbed down with her, and she accompanied him as he went to receive counseling and spiritual help. The following day the newspapers hailed Yolanda as a hero. But she would be the first to tell you that it was God who turned her illness—her liability—into an asset to save another life.

He does that all the time, usually in less spectacular ways. For those with physical or emotional scars—for those who have been beaten up by life or have endured relational wounds, God can open up opportunities to influence others who are going through a similar ordeal. And when he does that, it's an inspiring sight to behold and a satisfying mission to fulfill.

SCRIPTURES THAT HELP US TO LOOK AHEAD

There is surely a future hope for you, and your hope will not be cut off.

Proverbs 23:18

As for me, I watch in hope for the LORD, I wait for God my Savior; my God will hear me.

Micah 7:7

Paul wrote: "We always thank God, the Father of our Lord Jesus Christ, when we pray for you, because we have heard of your faith in Christ Jesus and of the love you have for all the saints—the faith and love that spring from the hope that is stored up for you in heaven and that you have already heard about in the word of truth, the gospel."

Colossians 1:3–5

Put your hope in the LORD both now and forevermore.

Psalm 131:3

Those who hope in the LORD will renew their strength. They will soar on wings like eagles; they will run and not grow weary, they will walk and not be faint.

Isaiah 40:31

Those who know your name will trust in you, for you, LORD, have never forsaken those who seek you.

Psalm 9:10

Yet if you devote your heart to God and stretch out your hands to him, . . . you will be secure, because there is hope; you will look about you and take your rest in safety.

Job 11:13,18

"For I know the plans I have for you," declares the LORD, "plans to prosper you and not to harm you, plans to give you hope and a future. Then you will call upon me and come and pray to me, and I will listen to you. You will seek me and find me when you seek me with all your heart."

Jeremiah 29:11–13

The LORD is good to those whose hope is in him, to the one who seeks him; it is good to wait quietly for the salvation of the LORD.

Lamentations 3:25–26

Know also that wisdom is sweet to your soul; if you find it, there is a future hope for you, and your hope will not be cut off.

Proverbs 24:14

It is God who arms me with strength and makes my way perfect. He makes my feet like the feet of a deer; he enables me to stand on the heights.

2 Samuel 22:33–34

Blessed is the man who trusts in the LORD, whose confidence is in him. He will be like a tree planted by the water that sends out its roots by the stream. It does not fear when heat comes; its leaves are always green. It has no worries in a year of drought and never fails to bear fruit.

Jeremiah 17:7–8

Do not fear, for I am with you; do not be dismayed, for I am your God. I will strengthen you and help you; I will uphold you with my righteous right hand.

Isaiah 41:10

For this is what the Sovereign LORD says, "I will search for the lost and bring back the strays. I will bind up the injured and strengthen the weak."

Ezekiel 34:11

You will keep in perfect peace him whose mind is steadfast, because he trusts in you, O LORD.

Isaiah 26:3

The LORD gives strength to his people; the LORD blesses his people with peace.

Psalm 29:11

I will listen to what God the LORD will say; he promises peace to his people, his saints.

Psalm 85:8

God will yet fill your mouth with laughter and your lips with shouts of joy.

Job 8:21

Many are asking, "Who can show us any good?" Let the light of your face shine upon us, O LORD. You have filled my heart with greater joy than when their grain and new wine abound.

Psalm 4:6–7

The LORD is good, a refuge in times of trouble. He cares for those who trust in him.

Nahum 1:7

I will lie down and sleep in peace, for you alone, O LORD, make me dwell in safety.

Psalm 4:8

Do not withhold your mercy from me, O LORD; may your love and your truth always protect me.

Psalm 40:11

Heal me, O LORD, and I will be healed; save me and I will be saved, for you are the one I praise.

Jeremiah 17:14

Even though I walk through the valley of the shadow of death, I will fear no evil, for you are with me, O God; your rod and your staff, they comfort me.

Psalm 23:4

As a mother comforts her child, so will God comfort you.

Isaiah 66:13

Be my rock of refuge, to which I can always go; give the command to save me, for you are my rock and my fortress.

Psalm 71:3

Look to the LORD and his strength; seek his face always.

1 Chronicles 16:11

Sustain me according to your promise, O LORD, and I will live; do not let my hopes be dashed.

Psalm 119:116

Be strong and take heart, all you who hope in the LORD.

Psalm 31:24

Do you not know? Have you not heard? The LORD is the everlasting God, the Creator of the ends of the earth. He will not grow tired or weary, and his understanding no one can fathom. He gives strength to the weary and increases the power of the weak.

Isaiah 40:28–29

Do not be anxious about anything, but in everything, by prayer and petition, with thanksgiving, present your requests to God. And the peace of God, which transcends all under-standing, will guard your hearts and your minds in Christ Jesus.

Philippians 4:6–7

But the Lord is faithful, and he will strengthen and protect you from the evil one.

2 Thessalonians 3:3

Shout for joy, O heavens; rejoice, O earth; burst into song, O mountains! For the LORD comforts his people and will have compassion on his afflicted ones.

Isaiah 49:13

From the ends of the earth I call to you, I call as my heart grows faint; lead me to the rock that is higher than I. For you have been my refuge, a strong tower against the foe.

Psalm 61:2–3

Find rest, O my soul, in God alone; my hope comes from him. He alone is my rock and my salvation; he is my fortress, I will not be shaken.

Psalm 62:5–6

The LORD is my strength and my shield; my heart trusts in him, and I am helped. My heart leaps for joy and I will give thanks to him in song. The LORD is the strength of his people, a fortress of salvation for his anointed one.

Psalm 28:7–8

LOOK
BEYOND

WHEN PAUL EXCLAIMED, "Where, O death, is your victory? Where, O death, is your sting?" (1 Corinthians 15:55), was he serious? How could he minimize death's devastating effects? Of course death stings. Just ask the widow, the orphan, the parents at the grave of their child. Death stings! . . . death stinks!

Every day brings fresh reminders of mortality—the slower step, the aches, the sickness, glasses, hearing aid, and pills. And though you know that death is the final destination for every person, that truth does not assuage your grief or

heal your pain in the cemetery. Instead, it seems to mock you as if to say, "You too will be here soon."

So there is a sting.

But Paul's words were not denying the reality of suffering. Instead, he was pointing to a greater reality—this life is not all there is. Beyond the grave is another life for the believer—life with God.

When you struggle, therefore, with the inevitability of death, look beyond. God promises eternal life to all who belong to him. TAKE HOPE.

SWEET BY AND BY

S.F. Bennett and J.P. Webster

THERE'S A LAND that is fairer than day,
And by faith, we can see it afar;
For the Father waits over the way,
To prepare us a dwelling place there.

In the sweet by and by,
We shall meet on that beautiful shore.
In the sweet by and by,
We shall meet on that beautiful shore.

We shall sing on that beautiful shore
The melodious songs of the blest,
And our spirits shall sorrow no more,
Not a sigh for the blessing of rest.

In the sweet by and by,
We shall meet on that beautiful shore.
In the sweet by and by,
We shall meet on that beautiful shore.

To our bountiful Father above
We will offer our tribute of praise,
For the glorious gift of His love
And the blessings that hallow our days.

In the sweet by and by,
We shall meet on that beautiful shore.
In the sweet by and by,
We shall meet on that beautiful shore.

MORE TO THE STORY
Barbara Johnson

DO YOU EVER have those days when everything in you groans out, "WHY BOTHER?" Why should I keep on trying . . . why should I stand up against the high tides of life . . . why should I stretch to love the unlovely . . . why should I keep hanging in there when no one appreciates my efforts and so few even know the sacrifices I've made . . . why should I put up with all this?!

I had a day like that recently. Over the holidays last year Bill and I met our son and his family for a fun gathering outside Seattle. Everything was going along great until Christmas night when the whole Northwest was slammed with an unbelievable ice storm. My plans to get home to Southern California the next day, where I had numerous deadlines to meet (and where it was warm!), went up in icicles.

For four days Bill and I were stuck in a small hotel room, far from where I "needed" to be, and a bit too close to hysteria as we watched two more storms barrel in. In between trips back and forth to the airport (which kept closing just as we'd pull up), I muttered to myself and used the sanity I had left to keep from spewing out my frustration to innocent onlookers—like the airline ticket agents and my husband.

Into my gloom and frustration, God sent a message of hope. In the mail the day before I'd left home, I'd received a tape from a pastor in Ohio whom I didn't even know. I'm not sure why I even plopped it and my Walkman into my suitcase because I have a lot of tapes lying around that I never find time to listen to. But God knew. In a voice full of assurance and victory, this pastor reminded me that "someday, the trumpet will sound and the dead will rise and we will be caught up to meet him in the skies!"

This life is not the end of the story! And my stay in the cramped hotel was oh, so temporary. However discouraged and beat up we may get here on earth, we can have joy in abundance because of what he promises us will be the outcome of our trials: finer character in this world and eternal joy in the next.

HEAVENLY THOUGHTS
Joni Eareckson Tada

"Hey, lady, your suitcase is over there!" a baggage handler yelled.
"Get that cart out of the way, would ya!"
"Taxi! Hey, stop—I said, 'Taxi!'" someone hollered outside.

It was mayhem. My friend was steering me in my wheelchair through thick crowds and piles of suitcases in the baggage claim area of the Los Angeles airport. Angry passengers bemoaned lost luggage. A line of people jostled through a turnstile. Outside, taxis honked. Policemen hollered. It was a crazy ending to an even crazier day of bad weather and a late arrival. We found our luggage carousel, and my friend parked my chair to go retrieve our things.

While I waited in the midst of pandemonium, I did what I always do. I waited and sat still. Very still. It's a fact of life. Because I'm paralyzed from the shoulders down, a large part of me never moves. I have instant stillness. I don't run, I sit. I don't race, I wait. Even when rushing, I stay put in my wheelchair. I could be scurrying through a jam-packed schedule, doing this and that, but a big part of me—due to my paralysis—is always quiet.

That's why, if you had seen me in that busy airport, you would have noticed a satisfied smile. Perhaps in an earlier time I would have felt trapped, useless, and resentful that I could not grab my own suitcase, elbow the guy who butted in line, or hail my own taxi. But faith, honed and sharpened from years in my wheelchair, has changed that. And so, I sat there thanking God for built-in quiet and stillness before Him. I also thought about heaven. With eyes of faith I looked beyond the sight of bumper-to-bumper traffic, the smell of sweat, cigarettes, exhaust fumes, and the sounds of my harried co-travelers, and began humming quietly . . .

This world is not my home, I'm just a passing through,
My treasures are laid up somewhere beyond the blue;
The angels beckon me from heaven's open door,
And I can't feel at home in this world anymore.

For me, it was a moment of faith. Faith merely the size of a grain of mustard seed. Remember, that's all it takes to be sure of things hoped for—future divine fulfillments—and certain of things you do not see, that is, unseen divine realities.

Of what was I so sure and certain? Here, let me sing it again:

The angels beckon me from heaven's open door,
And I can't feel at home in this world anymore.

HEAVEN'S OPEN DOOR

Dave and Jan Dravecky

AS CHILDREN OF GOD, we are citizens of
heaven. Earth is no longer our home; we long for
heaven. . . . Oh, how this conviction should
change the way we live right now! It did for
Jessica Eggert, a ten-year-old girl who was
diagnosed with osteogenic sarcoma, a rare cancer
that is fatal if not caught soon enough. In Jessica's
case, it wasn't. Her father tells the story:

I don't know exactly how Jessica came to
grasp the reality of heaven, but she certainly did.
It must have been in Sunday School that she
learned the truth of 2 Peter 3:8, "But do not forget
this one thing, dear friends: With the Lord a day
is like a thousand years, and a thousand years are
like a day." I think our talks about the deaths of
"Grandpa" Towne and "Grandma" Neva, "Papa"
Ed and "Grandma" Doe, the dear saints who had
befriended our children, added to her realization
that heaven is a very real place. I believe the
assurance of their presence in heaven did much
to remove her fear. She already knew people who
were in heaven and knew that they were waiting
for her.

By God's grace and many answered
prayers, Jessica lived with her cancer for three

and one-half years, although we had been told it would kill her within two to three months. Through her whole struggle—the horrible chemotherapy, the final weakening stage—her confidence in what lay ahead for her never wavered. I was amazed by how real heaven was to her. I was inspired by her complete peace. I found encouragement in her lack of fear or dread. Our hope, our comfort, and our strength for grieving were immeasurably enhanced by the powerful simplicity of her faith.

We will never forget our last evening with her. She was obviously near death and leaned across my chest. "I'm ready to go now, Daddy," she said. "Do you mean to heaven?" "Yes, Daddy. I'm ready to go over there." And go there she did, a few hours after slipping peacefully into a coma.

Jessica didn't feel at home in this world anymore, but she certainly felt at ease when a very unashamed God beckoned her to her new home in her new city and said joyfully, "Welcome home, Jessica. It just wouldn't be heaven without you."

TRANSFORMING LOVE

Joni Eareckson Tada

ON THE MORNING of the big day, my girlfriends laid me on a couch in the church's bridal salon to dress me. They strained and grunted to shift my paralyzed body this way and that, fitting me into the huge, cumbersome wedding gown. When I got back in my chair, an usher brought word that the guests were seated, and it was time to line up. We reached the glass doors of the church, they swung open, and the blast from the organ gave us goose bumps.

Just before the wedding march, I glanced down at my gown. I had accidentally wheeled over the hem. It left a greasy tire mark. My bouquet of daisies were off-center on my lap since my paralyzed hand couldn't hold them. No amount of corseting and binding my body gave me a perfect shape. The dress just didn't fit. It was draped over a thin wire mesh covering my wheels, but it still hung clumped and uneven. My chair was spiffed up as much as possible, but it was still the big, clunky gray thing with belts, gears, and ball bearings that it always was. I was not the picture-perfect bride you see in a magazine.

My last bridesmaid began her walk up the aisle, and I inched my chair closer to the last pew to catch a glimpse of Ken at the front. I saw him waiting at attention, looking tall and stately in his formal attire. He was craning his neck to look up the aisle. He was looking for me. My face grew hot and my heart began to pound. Suddenly, everything was different. I had seen my beloved. How I looked no longer mattered.

All that mattered was getting up to the front of the church to be with him. I could have felt ugly and unworthy, except that the love in Ken's face washed it all away. I was the pure and perfect bride. That's what he saw, and that's what changed me.

Years later, somewhere around our tenth wedding anniversary, I asked him, "What were you thinking on our wedding day?" His answer delighted me. He said, "I woke up so early that morning excited that I would get to see you in your wedding gown. And even though I knew there would be hundreds of people in the church, I knew my eyes would be for you only. In fact, I'll never forget that wonderful feeling when I saw you wheeling down the aisle in your chair. You looked so beautiful."

"You mean, you didn't think much about my wheelchair? My paralysis?" He thought for a minute, then shook his head. "No. Really, I just thought you were gorgeous." Our entrance into heaven may be something like this. One look from God will change us. And earth is just the dress rehearsal. True, we presently see stains and smudges all over us, and we cower, thinking, He'll never see anything lovely in me. But still, we ache to see Him.

One day He will come for us and look into our eyes. We will hold His gaze. And all the stains and smears of sin will be purified out of us just by one searching of those eyes. It will be more than we dreamed of, more than we longed for.

DANCING TOGETHER
Dave Dravecky

CORRIE TEN BOOM, whose story is told in *The Hiding Place*, survived Nazi concentration camps to go on to minister the gospel all over the world. Shortly before she went to be with the Lord, friends held a surprise "This is Your Life!" celebration in her honor. Everyone was trying to stay hidden so Corrie would not suspect anything, but she happened to run into Joni Eareckson Tada sitting in her wheelchair in a hallway. Joni is a quadriplegic who has ministered hope and encouragement to millions.

Corrie was frail by this time, her shoulders bent from age and the abuse she endured at the hands of the Nazis. She took Joni's hands in her wrinkled ones, leaned close to her, and whispered with her thick Dutch accent, "One day, Joni, you and I will dance together in heaven."

These two women have found the strength to live, the strength to suffer, and even the strength to face death with hope. Jesus Christ has given them the power within to cope with the decaying conditions of their bodies and the varying circumstances of life. One found that power in a Nazi death camp; the other found it sitting in a wheelchair.

They knew that the secret to living in hope, even though we may be broken in this life, is to know the promise of the resurrection. Jesus died a real death. He endured real pain. He was laid in a real tomb. He was raised in a real body to prove that death had really been conquered. He gave us real hope to believe that, just as he was raised from the dead, we too will be raised. We will be changed and our mortal bodies will put on immortality.

Like Corrie and Joni, we too will dance together in heaven. And what a glorious comeback that will be!

A HINT OF HEAVEN
Joni Eareckson Tada

ONE NIGHT, at a retreat, during the evening ice cream social, I powered my chair over to little red-haired Nicole in her wheelchair, Tiffany, her friend, and Rachel, standing next to her in her leg braces. After a couple of comments about the ice cream we were soon playing a game of tag. Wheelchair tag. Before long, a kid in a walker joined us with his sister. And then a child with Down's syndrome and her brother. Weaving in and out around the legs of the adults, we giggled and screamed as our foot pedals clunked together, bumping and bouncing like dodge'em cars.

After the ice cream began to melt, John, our retreat director, looked at his watch and tried to herd the families back to their cabins. But we kept playing. We were so caught up in the game that I lost all track of time. Only after we waved goodnight to each other, exhausted, did I realize it was like heaven. It was heaven because of the play and the joy and the sense of timelessness. Right before I entered my cabin, I looked up to the stars and thanked Jesus for the sneak preview of heaven's joy. I had to smile at His answer from Matthew 19:14: "Let the little children come to me . . . for the kingdom of heaven belongs to such as these."

As I laid in bed that night, the entire experience of joyful play kept echoing. The kingdom of heaven belongs to giggling, happy, carefree children. I kept thinking and straining my ears—or was I trying to open the eyes of my heart—to hear or see more. I knew there was much more than just play in that experience. I had touched a moment of great happiness and wisdom. I didn't realize it then, but I had touched eternity in time.

A Place to Stake Your Hope
Philip Yancey

IN OCTOBER OF 1988 one of my closest friends died in a scuba diving accident in Lake Michigan. The very afternoon Bob was making his last dive I was sitting, oblivious, in a university coffee shop reading *My Quest for Beauty*, a book by the famous therapist and author Rollo May. The book tells of Rollo May's lifelong search for beauty, and among the experiences he recounts is a visit to Mt. Athos, a peninsula of Greece inhabited exclusively by monks.

Rollo May was beginning to recover from a nervous breakdown when he visited Mt. Athos. He happened to arrive just as the monks were celebrating Greek Orthodox Easter, a ceremony thick with symbolism, thick with beauty. Icons were everywhere. Incense hung in the air. And at the height of that service the priest gave everyone present three Easter eggs, wonderfully decorated and wrapped in a veil. "Christos Anesti!" he said—"Christ is risen!" Each person there, including Rollo May, responded according to custom, "He is risen indeed!"

Rollo May was not a believer. But he writes in his book, "I was seized then by a moment of spiritual reality: what would it mean for our world if He had truly risen?" I returned home shortly after reading that chapter, and was met at the door by my wife who conveyed the news of Bob's death. Rollo May's question came back to me many times in the next few days. What does it mean for the world if Christ has truly risen?

I spoke at my friend's funeral, and there I asked Rollo May's question in a different way, in the context of the grief that pressed in on us from all sides. What would it mean for us if Bob rose again? We sat in a chapel, numbed by three days of sadness. I imagined aloud what it would be like to walk outside to the parking lot and there, to our utter amazement, find Bob. Bob! With his bounding walk, his big grin, and clear gray eyes.

That conjured image gave me a hint of what Jesus' disciples felt on Easter Sunday. They too had grieved for three days. But on Sunday they caught a glimpse of something else, a glimpse of the future.

Apart from Easter, apart from a new start, a recreated earth—apart from

all that, we could indeed judge God less-than-powerful or less-than-loving or even cruel. The Bible stakes God's reputation on his ability to restore creation to its original state of perfection.

I confess that I too used to be embarrassed by talk about heaven and an afterlife. It seemed a cop-out, a crutch. We ought to make our way in the world as if that is all there is, I thought. But I've watched people die. What kind of God would be satisfied forever with a world like this one, laden with suffering and death? If I had to stand by and watch lives like Bob's get cut off—suddenly vanish, vaporize—with no hope of a future, I doubt I'd believe in God.

A passage in the New Testament, 1 Corinthians 15, expresses much the same thought. Paul first reviews his life, a difficult life that included jailing, beatings, shipwrecks, and gladiator-style contests with wild beasts. Then he says, in so many words, I'd be crazy to go through all this if it ended at my death. "If only for this life we have hope in Christ, we are to be pitied more than all men." Along with Paul, I stake my hope on resurrection, a time when Christ "will transform our lowly bodies so that they will be like his glorious body" (Philippians 3:21).

If Heaven Means Anything

Dave and Jan Dravecky

LORRIE SHAVER WAS NOT SPECTACULAR in appearance. She was overweight and wore, for the most part, pullover shirts, corduroy jeans, and work boots. Her hands were sliced and stained and calloused, fingernails short and stubby—the hands of a girl who worked with boxes at a Florida grocery store. Her eyes were small, and she had freckles.

The same is true of her actions: nothing spectacular. She never saved anyone from drowning; she worked hard for grades at college; she wasn't creative, she had few original ideas.

"She was as average a girl as they come," says her pastor, Paul Mutchler. "She was totally vanilla. There were no special gifts or talents—except for one. And that was love. She loved people specifically, and that made her very special."

More than anything, Lorrie Shaver wanted to do some small thing for the Lord. Kent and Becky Good, who grew up in her home church, were missionaries to France. She began to seek them out. "During missions conference I stayed in Lorrie's dorm room," says Becky Good. "She began asking me some serious questions about France. Could she be used as a missionary?" Becky remembers one conversation lasting until two in the morning. Later, Lorrie went to France to attend the Euro-Missions Conference. While attending the conference, she saw the tremendous spiritual need in the country. By the time the conference had ended she had made a decision: She wanted to be a missionary in France.

A few weeks before she was to leave for France, Lorrie was to be commissioned as a missionary at a conference in Colorado. She booked a plane for Denver with a layover in Dallas.

The phone rang in Patty Bender's house about 10 p.m., August 2, 1985. It startled her out of a nap. She fought the slow haze that follows half-sleep. The television pulsating impossible shadows; the movie she couldn't remember; the kids were in bed.

She heard her husband, Phil, answer the phone: "Oh, hi!" She knew, by the tone of his voice, it was her mom. Probably just wanted to chat. Phil wasn't talking a lot, just uh-huhs and yeahs. "Let me have the phone," Patty said. Her husband said no.

"Okay," he said into the phone, "we'll talk to you tomorrow." He hung up.

"What's wrong?" Patty asked. "Lorrie's been in a plane accident" was the answer. "We don't know if she's a survivor or not."

After the phone call, Patty Bender was hysterical. They watched the news—an L-1011, Delta Flight 191, had crashed in Dallas. The pictures were horrible. The only survivors, the anchor man dead-panned, were in the smoking section. Patty got mad, real mad. She had lost a lifetime friend. Her husband tried to comfort her; he prayed.

"I kept screaming 'why?' Why could God let this happen to Lorrie? She was getting ready to go to France and serve Him as a missionary. Why? How could God do this?"

It wasn't that Patty didn't believe the answer—heaven. The answer wasn't the problem, the question was. . . . After the memorial service, Patty Bender went to the Shaver's house. The service was standing room only; now it was only a handful of Lorrie's closest friends. They reminisced until nearly midnight. They laughed and laughed. During the evening, Patty, for the first time, was joyful. "It was there that it hit me—Lorrie's in heaven," Patty says. "And heaven meant something to me then."

Patty still couldn't explain the whys. Obedience, sometimes, just didn't make sense. She knew that her friend's death had changed her: "She taught me what was really important in life." And as the sound of laughter filtered through a Florida summer night, so did Patty's anger.

YOUNG AND OLD

Philip Yancey

J. ROBERTSON MCQUILKIN, former president of Columbia Bible College, was once approached by an elderly lady facing the trials of old age. Her body was in decline, her beauty being replaced by thinning hair, wrinkles, and skin discoloration. She could no longer do the things she once could, and she felt herself to be a burden on others. "Robertson, why does God let us get old and weak? Why must I hurt so?" she asked.

After a few moments' thought McQuilkin replied, "I think God has planned the strength and beauty of youth to be physical. But the strength and beauty of age is spiritual. We gradually lose the strength and beauty that is temporary so we'll be sure to concentrate on the strength and beauty which is forever. It makes us more eager to leave behind the temporary, deteriorating part of us and be truly homesick for our eternal home. If we stayed young and beautiful, we might never want to leave!"

If there is a secret to handling suffering, the one most often cited is along this line. To survive, the spirit must be fed so that it can break free beyond the constraints of the body. Christian faith does not always offer resources to the body.

"Do not be afraid of those who can only kill your body; they cannot kill your soul," Jesus said as he sent out his followers. Because physical death is not the end, we need not fear it inordinately. But because it is the enemy of Life, we need not welcome it either.

In short, because of our belief in a home beyond, Christians can be realistic about death without becoming hopeless. Death is an enemy, but a defeated enemy. As Martin Luther told his followers, "Even in the best of health we should have death always before our eyes so that we will not expect to remain on this earth forever, but will have one foot in the air, so to speak."

ACORNS AND OAKS
Joni Eareckson Tada

YOU DO NOT PLANT the body that will be. I learned this lesson on one of those blustery November afternoons when I tend to get thoughtful and meditative. I glanced outside my window and spied a fat, furry squirrel doing his autumn ritual of collecting acorns. I watched him sniff each one, inspecting them in his paws, then stuffing his cheeks with the tastiest nuts. Others he dropped on the ground.

The acorns he discarded rolled around in the stiff breeze. I knew most of them would blow away. Others would remain on the dirt to dry in the chilly air. And a few, just a few, would take root under the soil. They would be the ones next season to sprout forth green shoots of new life. These were the acorns destined to be trees.

I shook my head in amazement. If you were to tell that tiny acorn that one day he would be as tall as a building with heavy branches and thick, green leaves, a tree so great it would house many squirrels, that nut would say you were crazy. A gigantic oak tree bears absolutely no resemblance to an acorn. The two, although related, seem as different as night and day.

Somehow, somewhere within that acorn is the promise and pattern of the tree it will become. Somehow, somewhere within you is the pattern of the heavenly person you will become, and if you want to catch a glimpse of how glorious and full of splendor your body will be, just do a comparison. Compare a hairy peach pit with the tree it becomes, loaded with fragrant blossoms and sweet fruit. They are totally different, yet the same. Compare a caterpillar with a butterfly. A wet, musty flower bulb with an aromatic hyacinth. A hairy coconut with a graceful palm tree.

It's no wonder you and I get stymied thinking about our resurrection bodies; whether or not our teeth will be straight or our digestive systems intact. First Corinthians 15:42–44 only touches on it: "The body that is sown is perishable, it is raised imperishable; it is sown in dishonor, it is raised in glory; it is sown in weakness, it is raised in power; it is sown a natural body, it is raised a spiritual body." It is sown . . . it is raised. We may not be

able to describe the changes, but we know it's the same "it." You and what you will one day be are one and the same—yet different.

Trying to understand what our bodies will be like in heaven is much like expecting an acorn to understand its destiny of roots, bark, branches, and leaves. Or asking a caterpillar to appreciate flying. Or a peach pit to fathom being fragrant. Or a coconut to grasp what it means to sway in the ocean breeze. Our eternal bodies will be so grand, so glorious, that we can only catch a fleeting glimpse of the splendor to come. C.S. Lewis marveled: "It is a serious thing to live in a society of possible gods and goddesses."

Lima beans. Kernels of wheat. Peach pits. Acorns and oak trees. Examples in nature are what the Bible invites us to use since "what we will be has not yet been made known" (1 John 3:2). One of the best ways to understand the resurrection is to take a field trip after the apostle Paul's lesson in nature: Go find an acorn on the ground, look up into the billowy skirts of the green from which it fell, and then praise God that "so it will be with the resurrection of the dead."

Can you now see why I enjoy dreaming about heaven?

FOR WHOM THE BELL TOLLS

Philip Yancey

JOHN DONNE, a seventeenth-century poet, found himself listening to the megaphone of pain. An angry father-in-law got him fired from his job and blackballed from a career in law. Donne turned in desperation to the church, taking orders as an Anglican priest. But that year after he took his first parish job, his wife Anne died, leaving him seven children. And a few years later, in 1623, spots appeared on Donne's own body. He was diagnosed with the bubonic plague.

The illness dragged on, sapping his strength almost to the point of death. (Donne's illness turned out to be a form of typhus, not the plague.) In the midst of this illness, Donne wrote a series of devotions on suffering which rank among the most poignant meditations ever written on the subject. He composed the book in bed, without benefit of notes, convinced he was dying.

In *Devotions*, John Donne calls God to task. As he looks back on life, it doesn't make sense. After spending a lifetime in confused wandering, he has finally reached a place where he can be of some service to God, and now, at that precise moment, he is struck by a deadly illness. Nothing appears on the horizon but fever, pain, and death. What to make of it?

What is the meaning of disease? John Donne's book suggests the possibility of an answer. The first stirrings came to him through the open window of his bedroom, in the form of church bells tolling out a doleful declaration of death. For an instant Donne wondered if his friends, knowing his condition to be more grave than they had disclosed, had ordered the bell to be rung for his own death. But he quickly realized that the bells were marking a neighbor's death from the plague.

Donne wrote Meditation XVII on the meaning of the church bells, one of the most celebrated passages in English literature ("No man is an island . . . Never send to know for whom the bell tolls; it tolls for thee"). He realized that although the bells had been sounded in honor of another's death, they served as a stark reminder of what every human being spends a lifetime trying to forget: We will die.

When one man dies, one chapter is not torn out of the book, but translated into a better language; and every chapter must be so translated; God employs several translators; some pieces are translated by age, some by sickness, some by war, some by justice; but God's hand is in every translation, and his hand shall bind up all our scattered leaves again for that library where every book shall lie open to one another. . . . So this bell calls us all.

ON OUR WAY HOME

Joni Eareckson Tada

I LIKE EARTH. But my heart pumps for heaven.

Calabasa, California, is nice, but it pales in the light of the heavenly realms. Home is pretty good here, but my homing instincts often have me pulling up a chair on the front porch of my mansion to shade my eyes and scan "a land that stretches afar." I have a glorious homesickness for heaven, a penetrating and piercing ache. I'm a stranger in a strange land, a displaced person with a fervent and passionate pain that is, oh, so satisfying. The groans are a blessing. What a sweetness to feel homesick for heaven, for "a longing fulfilled is sweet to the soul" (Proverbs 13:19).

Never was this symbolized more clearly than at one of our recent JAF Ministries' retreats I helped lead for families of disabled children. After a week of wheelchair hikes, Bible studies, and arts and crafts, I listened as the microphone was passed from family to family, each tearfully sharing how wonderful the time had been. Some talked of meeting new friends. Others, of the games, music, and hikes. A few said how they wished the week could go on and on.

Then little red-haired, freckle-faced Jeff raised his hand. He had Down's syndrome and had won the hearts of many adults at the retreat. People had been captivated by his winsome smile and joyful spirit. Everyone leaned forward to hear his words. Jeff grabbed the mike and kept it short and sweet as he bellowed: "Let's go home!" He smiled, bowed, and handed back the microphone. All the families roared with laughter.

His mother told me later that, even though Jeff immersed himself in the week's festivities, he missed his daddy back home.

I identify with Jeff. The good things in this world are pleasant enough, but would we really wish for it to go on as it is? I don't think so. The nice things in this life are merely omens of even greater, more glorious things yet to come. God would not have us mistake this world for a permanent dwelling. It was C.S. Lewis who

said something about not mistaking pleasant inns for home on our journey to heaven. I'm with him and I'm with Jeff. It's a good life, but I am looking forward to going home.

    I miss my home. I miss God.

SCRIPTURES THAT HELP US TO LOOK BEYOND

But store up for yourselves treasures in heaven, where moth and rust do not destroy, and where thieves do not break in and steal. For where your treasure is, there your heart will be also.

Matthew 6:20–21

There are also heavenly bodies and there are earthly bodies; but the splendor of the heavenly bodies is one kind, and the splendor of the earthly bodies is another.

1 Corinthians 15:40

So will it be with the resurrection of the dead. The body that is sown is perishable, it is raised imperishable; it is sown in dishonor, it is raised in glory; it is sown in weakness, it is raised in power; it is sown a natural body, it is raised a spiritual body.

1 Corinthians 15:42–44

Dear friends, now we are children of God, and what we will be has not yet been made known. But we know that when he appears, we shall be like him, for we shall see him as he is. Everyone who has this hope in Christ purifies himself, just as he is pure.

1 John 3:2–3

Now we know that if the earthly tent we live in is destroyed, we have a building from God, an eternal house in heaven, not built by human hands. Meanwhile we groan, longing to be clothed with our heavenly dwelling, because when we are clothed, we will not be found naked. For while we are in this tent, we groan and are burdened, because we do not wish to be unclothed but to be clothed with our heavenly dwelling, so that what is mortal may be swallowed up by life. Now it is God who has made us for this very purpose and has given us the Spirit as a deposit, guaranteeing what is to come.

2 Corinthians 5:1–5

When the perishable has been clothed with the imperishable, and the mortal with immortality, then the saying that is written will come true: "Death has been swallowed up in victory." "Where, O death, is your victory? Where, O death, is your sting?" The sting of death is sin, and the power of sin is the law. But thanks be to God! He gives us the victory through our Lord Jesus Christ.

1 Corinthians 15:54–57

Then I saw a new heaven and a new earth, for the first heaven and the first earth had passed away, and there was no longer any sea. I saw the Holy City, the new Jerusalem, coming down out of heaven from God, prepared as a bride beautifully dressed for her husband. And I heard a loud voice from the throne saying, "Now the dwelling of God is with men, and he will live with them. They will be his people, and God himself will be with them and be their God. He will wipe every tear from their eyes. There will be no more death or mourning or crying or pain, for the old order of things has passed away."

Revelation 21:1–4

I pray also that the eyes of your heart may be enlightened in order that you may know the hope to which God has called you, the riches of his glorious inheritance in the saints, and his incomparably great power for us who believe.

Ephesians 1:18–19

For the kingdom of God is not a matter of eating and drinking, but of righteousness, peace and joy in the Holy Spirit.

Romans 14:17

Praise be to the God and Father of our Lord Jesus Christ, who has blessed us in the heavenly realms with every spiritual blessing in Christ.

Ephesians 1:3

No one whose hope is in God will ever be put to shame.

Psalm 25:3

We have confidence to enter the Most Holy Place by the blood of Jesus. Let us draw near to God with a sincere heart in full assurance of faith. Let us hold unswervingly to the hope we profess, for he who promised is faithful.

Hebrews 10:19,22–23

If anyone is in Christ, he is a new creation; the old has gone, the new has come! God made him who had no sin to be sin for us, so that in him we might become the righteousness of God.

2 Corinthians 5:17,21

As the deer pants for streams of water, so my soul pants for you, O God. My soul thirsts for God, for the living God. When can I go and meet with God?

Psalm 42:1–2

God's people will live in peaceful dwelling places, in secure homes, in undisturbed places of rest.

Isaiah 32:18

Fear not, for I have redeemed you; I have summoned you by name; you are mine. When you pass through the waters, I will be with you; and when you pass through the rivers, they will not sweep over you. When you walk through the fire, you will not be burned; the flames will not set you ablaze. For I am the LORD, your God, the Holy One of Israel, your Savior.

Isaiah 43:1–3

May the Lord strengthen your hearts so that you will be blameless and holy in the presence of our God and Father when our Lord Jesus comes with all his holy ones.

1 Thessalonians 3:13

Wait for the LORD; be strong and take heart and wait for the LORD.

Psalm 27:14

This is what the LORD says—"Forget the former things; do not dwell on the past. See, I am doing a new thing! Now it springs up; do you not perceive it? I am making a way in the desert and streams in the wasteland."

Isaiah 43:16,18–19

SOURCES

The Blessings of Brokenness by Charles Stanley. Copyright 1997 by Charles F. Stanley.

Bring Back the Joy by Sheila Walsh. Copyright 1998 by Sheila Walsh and New Life Clinics, d.b.a. Women of Faith.

Descending Into Greatness by Bill Hybels and Rob Wilkins. Copyright 1993 by Bill Hybels.

Do Not Lose Heart by Dave and Jan Dravecky with Steve Halliday. Copyright 1998 by David and Janice Dravecky.

God's Outrageous Claims by Lee Strobel. Copyright 1997 by Lee Strobel.

Heaven, Your Real Home by Joni Eareckson Tada. Copyright 1995 by Joni Eareckson Tada.

Joni by Joni Eareckson Tada and Joe Musser. Copyright 1976 by Joni Eareckson Tada and Joe Musser.

Joy Breaks by Patsy Clairmont, Barbara Johnson, Marilyn Meberg, Luci Swindoll. Copyright 1997 by New Life Clinics.

The Joyful Journey by Patsy Clairmont, Barbara Johnson, Marilyn Meberg, Luci Swindoll. Copyright 1997 by New Life Clinics.

Outrageous Joy by Patsy Clairmont, Barbara Johnson, Marilyn Meberg, Luci Swindoll, Sheila Walsh, Thelma Wells. Copyright 1999 by Women of Faith, Inc.

Overjoyed! by Patsy Clairmont, Barbara Johnson, Marilyn Meberg, Luci Swindoll, Sheila Walsh, Thelma Wells. Copyright 1999 by Women of Faith, Inc.

Loving God by Charles W. Colson. Copyright 1983, 1987 by Charles W. Colson.

Where is God when it Hurts? by Philip Yancey. Copyright 1977, 1990 by Philip Yancey.

Worth of a Man by Dave Dravecky with Connie Neal. Copyright 1996 by David F. Dravecky.